WINDY DRYDEN was b
worked in psychotherap
seventeen years and is the
books, including *Counsell*
Emotive Approach (1987,
Questions Answered (1989), co-authored with Martin
Cole. Dr Dryden is Senior Lecturer in Psychology at
Goldsmiths' College, University of London.

JACK GORDON was born in Dundee in 1921. After
working for many years in a variety of management jobs
he trained in Rational-Emotive Therapy, and now
intends to devote his life to popularizing RET through
writing and speaking.

Windy Dryden and Jack Gordon are also the authors of
Think Your Way to Happiness (Sheldon 1990).

Overcoming Common Problems Series

For a full list of titles please contact
Sheldon Press, Marylebone Road, London NW1 4DU

Beating Job Burnout
DR DONALD SCOTT

Beating the Blues
SUSAN TANNER AND JILLIAN
BALL

Being the Boss
STEPHEN FITZSIMON

Birth Over Thirty
SHEILA KITZINGER

Body Language
How to read others' thoughts by their
gestures
ALLAN PEASE

Bodypower
DR VERNON COLEMAN

Bodysense
DR VERNON COLEMAN

Calm Down
How to cope with frustration and anger
DR PAUL HAUCK

Changing Course
How to take charge of your career
SUE DYSON AND STEPHEN HOARE

Comfort for Depression
JANET HORWOOD

Complete Public Speaker
GYLES BRANDRETH

**Coping Successfully with Your Child's
Asthma**
DR PAUL CARSON

**Coping Successfully with Your Hyperactive
Child**
DR PAUL CARSON

**Coping Successfully with Your Irritable
Bowel**
ROSEMARY NICOL

Coping with Anxiety and Depression
SHIRLEY TRICKETT

Coping with Blushing
DR ROBERT EDELMANN

Coping with Cot Death
SARAH MURPHY

Coping with Depression and Elation
DR PATRICK McKEON

Coping with Stress
DR GEORGIA WITKIN-LANOIL

Coping with Suicide
DR DONALD SCOTT

Coping with Thrush
CAROLINE CLAYTON

Curing Arthritis – The Drug-Free Way
MARGARET HILLS

Curing Arthritis Diet Book
MARGARET HILLS

**Curing Coughs, Colds and Flu – The
Drug-Free Way**
MARGARET HILLS

Curing Illness – The Drug-Free Way
MARGARET HILLS

Depression
DR PAUL HAUCK

Divorce and Separation
ANGELA WILLANS

Don't Blame Me!
How to stop blaming yourself
and other people
TONY GOUGH

The Epilepsy Handbook
SHELAGH McGOVERN

**Everything You Need to Know about
Adoption**
MAGGIE JONES

**Everything You Need to Know about
Contact Lenses**
DR ROBERT YOUNGSON

**Everything You Need to Know about
Osteoporosis**
ROSEMARY NICOL

Overcoming Common Problems Series

Everything You Need to Know about Shingles
DR ROBERT YOUNGSON

Everything You Need to Know about Your Eyes
DR ROBERT YOUNGSON

Family First Aid and Emergency Handbook
DR ANDREW STANWAY

Feverfew
A traditional herbal remedy for migraine and arthritis
DR STEWART JOHNSON

Fight Your Phobia and Win
DAVID LEWIS

Getting Along with People
DIANNE DOUBTFIRE

Getting Married
JOANNA MOORHEAD

Goodbye Backache
DR DAVID IMRIE WITH COLLEEN DIMSON

Heart Attacks – Prevent and Survive
DR TOM SMITH

Helping Children Cope with Divorce
ROSEMARY WELLS

Helping Children Cope with Grief
ROSEMARY WELLS

Helping Children Cope with Stress
URSULA MARKHAM

Hold Your Head Up High
DR PAUL HAUCK

How to be a Successful Secretary
SUE DYSON AND STEPHEN HOARE

How to Be Your Own Best Friend
DR PAUL HAUCK

How to Control your Drinking
DRS W. MILLER AND R. MUNOZ

How to Cope with Stress
DR PETER TYRER

How to Cope with Tinnitus and Hearing Loss
DR ROBERT YOUNGSON

How to Cope with Your Child's Allergies
DR PAUL CARSON

How to Cure Your Ulcer
ANNE CHARLISH AND DR BRIAN GAZZARD

How to Do What You Want to Do
DR PAUL HAUCK

How to Get Things Done
ALISON HARDINGHAM

How to Improve Your Confidence
DR KENNETH HAMBLY

How to Interview and Be Interviewed
MICHELE BROWN AND GYLES BRANDRETH

How to Love a Difficult Man
NANCY GOOD

How to Love and be Loved
DR PAUL HAUCK

How to Make Successful Decisions
ALISON HARDINGHAM

How to Move House Successfully
ANNE CHARLISH

How to Pass Your Driving Test
DONALD RIDLAND

How to Say No to Alcohol
KEITH McNEILL

How to Spot Your Child's Potential
CECILE DROUIN AND ALAIN DUBOS

How to Stand up for Yourself
DR PAUL HAUCK

How to Start a Conversation and Make Friends
DON GABOR

How to Stop Smoking
GEORGE TARGET

How to Stop Taking Tranquillisers
DR PETER TYRER

How to Stop Worrying
DR FRANK TALLIS

How to Study Successfully
MICHELE BROWN

Overcoming Common Problems Series

Hysterectomy
SUZIE HAYMAN

Jealousy
DR PAUL HAUCK

Learning from Experience
A woman's guide to getting
older without panic
PATRICIA O'BRIEN

Learning to Live with Multiple Sclerosis
DR ROBERT POVEY, ROBIN DOWIE
AND GILLIAN PRETT

Living Alone – A Woman's Guide
LIZ McNEILL TAYLOR

Living Through Personal Crisis
ANN KAISER STEARNS

Living with Grief
DR TONY LAKE

Living with High Blood Pressure
DR TOM SMITH

Loneliness
DR TONY LAKE

Making Marriage Work
DR PAUL HAUCK

Making the Most of Loving
GILL COX AND SHEILA DAINOW

Making the Most of Yourself
GILL COX AND SHEILA DAINOW

Managing Two Careers
How to survive as a working mother
PATRICIA O'BRIEN

Meeting People is Fun
How to overcome shyness
DR PHYLLIS SHAW

Menopause
RAEWYN MACKENZIE

The Nervous Person's Companion
DR KENNETH HAMBLY

Overcoming Fears and Phobias
DR TONY WHITEHEAD

Overcoming Shyness
A woman's guide
DIANNE DOUBTFIRE

Overcoming Stress
DR VERNON COLEMAN

Overcoming Tension
DR KENNETH HAMBLY

Overcoming Your Nerves
DR TONY LAKE

The Parkinson's Disease Handbook
DR RICHARD GODWIN-AUSTEN

Say When!
Everything a woman needs to know about
alcohol and drinking problems
ROSEMARY KENT

Self-Help for your Arthritis
EDNA PEMBLE

Slay Your Own Dragons
How women can overcome
self-sabotage in love and work
NANCY GOOD

Sleep Like a Dream – The Drug-Free Way
ROSEMARY NICOL

Solving your Personal Problems
PETER HONEY

A Special Child in the Family
Living with your sick or disabled child
DIANA KIMPTON

Think Your Way to Happiness
DR WINDY DRYDEN AND JACK GORDON

Trying to Have a Baby?
Overcoming infertility and child loss
MAGGIE JONES

Why Be Afraid?
How to overcome your fears
DR PAUL HAUCK

Women and Depression
A practical self-help guide
DEIDRE SANDERS

You and Your Varicose Veins
DR PATRICIA GILBERT

Your Arthritic Hip and You
GEORGE TARGET

Your Grandchild and You
ROSEMARY WELLS

Overcoming Common Problems

HOW TO UNTANGLE
YOUR EMOTIONAL KNOTS

Windy Dryden and Jack Gordon

SHELDON PRESS
LONDON

First published in Great Britain in 1991
Sheldon Press, SPCK, Marylebone Road, London NW1 4DU

British Library Cataloguing in Publication Data
Dryden, Windy
  1. How to untangle your emotional knots.
  I. Title   II. Gordon, Jack *1921–*
  152.41

  ISBN 0–85969–631–6

Typeset by Deltatype Ltd, Ellesmere Port, Cheshire
Printed in Great Britain by Biddles Ltd, Guildford and Kings Lynn

Contents

Introduction   1

1   Fundamental Ideas   5

2   'A Good Man Is Hard to Find'   22

3   'I Can't Face the Risk of Rejection'   43

4   'I Just Get Jealous and I Don't Know Why'   60

5   'He Treats Me Like a Doormat'   78

6   'He Makes Me So Angry'   98

7   Working It Out or Giving It Up   116

Introduction

Why we decided to write this book

If you were asked to name the subject that probably attracts the attention of more people more of the time than any other subject in modern times, what would it be? Politics? Or maybe pop music? Both of these may well come close, but our guess would be *love*. For a start, where would pop music be without it? Without love to dream about, to cry over, to die for, to demand for eternity, the charts would all but disappear. And other kinds of music are so dependent upon the theme of love that without it they would never have been written. Can you imagine Gershwin, Cole Porter or Irving Berlin turning out those melodies for which they became famous without at least a nod in the direction of love? Without the tragedies often associated with love, even inspired by it, some of our most famous operas could never have been written. And the same could be said for much of our literature, especially poetry.

As if all that were not enough, look at the enormous amount of time and effort devoted to the problems of love! Phone-ins, chat lines, articles galore in popular newspapers and magazines are full of advice and reassurance to the lovelorn. One columnist writing for a well-known national daily was quoted as saying that she received a thousand letters a week from readers with problems about their love relationships!

You might well ask, in view of this vast outpouring of human resources on the subject, what we can possibly hope to achieve by contributing yet another book on the subject. Hasn't enough already been said and written to last us all a lifetime? Well, we admit there is certainly enough material available, maybe even too much. So, are we dissatisfied with the quality of the advice so widely offered to the perplexed through the various media? Not necessarily. Much of the advice proffered is sensible, practical and potentially helpful, *if acted upon*. Good sane, down-to-earth stuff, which, *if followed through*, would benefit the recipient; the sort of advice we would give some of our own clients. But *is* it acted upon? How many of those in some kind of emotional turmoil who write or phone in for help actually know *how* to carry out the wise counsel they receive? The answer is, pretty few! And *that* is why we have written this book: to show you how to use whatever help you are offered to overcome your love and relationship problems.

1

There are no ready-made answers

Most emphatically, what we are *not* going to do is to offer you a set of off-the-shelf answers to some of the most common problems of love. There are two reasons why not: first, although there are only a limited number of ways you can feel upset about a problem with love, you are a unique person in a unique set of circumstances. Your situation is different from that of someone else even if you both have the same problem. It follows that the solution to your problem must take into consideration your own particular situation. This may embrace your home, your workplace or some other set of relationships specific to you which are not necessarily applicable to someone else with a similar problem.

Our second and more important reason for not fobbing you off with standard answers to common problems is that you will reap far more benefit if we can show you how to solve your problems for yourself, either by using your own common sense or, if you need to, by seeking professional advice. And if your particular problem is, for the time being, not amenable to a practical solution – as, alas, some are not – just knowing how to think about your problem will enable you to live with the situation until a practical solution does become feasible, *and* with a great deal less wear and tear on your nervous system.

We have something special to offer you

What we are going to do is teach you a new way of looking at things: a new way of thinking about yourself, your emotions and your inter-personal relationships. The credit for this goes to Dr Albert Ellis, a famous clinical psychologist in New York who originated this new way of thinking, and developed the ideas on which it is based into an effective system of psychotherapy. Known as *Rational-Emotive Therapy*, or RET for short, it's a system which has been researched, developed and tested in practice over three decades by thousands of mental health practitioners around the world, including ourselves, and is recognized today as one of the most effective ways known of enabling people to overcome their emotional problems and lead more satisfying lives. As you learn how to use RET, you will come to see how it provides a framework for understanding and solving virtually any emotional difficulty you may experience – especially problems with love.

Who are we writing for?

We are writing mainly for women, but with men in mind. Men frequently create problems for women in relationships and contribute to the resulting emotional problems experienced by women, and sometimes by their partners as well. We are not suggesting it is one-sided. Sometimes women create problems for their men. But it does seem that women are more often on the receiving end.

What we hope to achieve

Both sexes can benefit from learning better ways to relate to each other. Our aim is to show people how to apply our problem-solving techniques to their love and relationship problems, so that both sexes can lead happier, more fulfilling lives. If that's what you want, this practical, down-to-earth guide will put you in the driving seat.

1
Fundamental Ideas

There is a widespread conviction that our feelings are created inside us by external events as well as by the words and actions of other people with whom we come into contact. A recent TV documentary on the ineffectiveness of current legislation in Britain to enable female victims of sexual harassment to obtain compensation through the courts claimed that the legal procedures involved in pressing a case were experienced by the women involved as every bit as unpleasant and 'degrading' as the harassment itself. One woman confessed that she was made to feel 'cheap' while presenting her evidence. It is well known that, in cases of rape, many women are loath to press charges because of the imputations against their character made by defending counsel and sometimes by the police themselves, who can appear to the unfortunate victims as unsympathetic or even hostile. Women in these circumstances describe themselves as 'ashamed', 'worthless', 'soiled' and 'degraded'. These are genuine feelings, as anyone who has undergone such experiences will readily confirm – it all seems so obvious, doesn't it? A sharp knife can cut you and cause you to feel pain. So shouldn't sharp, cutting words or hostile actions make you feel pain, too? Or anger? We will show you now that it is not quite as simple as that.

The A-B-C of emotional disturbance

Let's suppose that you have been the object of sexual harassment in the office where you work and you go into your boss's office and lodge a formal complaint. Your boss is not very sympathetic. He tries to play down the various episodes you bring to his attention. You persist, so your boss insinuates that you really invited the harassment. He tells you that you dress 'provocatively' and that men could hardly be blamed for propositioning you. He implies that you, and women like you, are only out for what you can get, and are a disruptive force in any office. Suppose we call your interview with the boss 'point A'. As you leave his office you feel angry and humiliated. Let's call this emotional conse-quence 'point C'. So, we have an activating event, which we call point A, which in this case stands for what your boss said to you at the interview. At point C, we have an emotional consequence, which in this case consists of shame, humiliation and anger. You probably think that A caused C. The boss's attitude and words, which implied that you

5

were really a bit of a tart, *made* you feel hurt and angry. Most people would agree with you: A caused C. Right? *Wrong*!

Well, if A doesn't cause C, what does? The answer is B! Point B stands for your belief system; it stands for what you basically believe about the world and how you evaluate and appraise what is happening to you. Expressions such as 'This is good', 'I don't like that', 'I can't stand it', are all examples of evaluative statements which reflect what you really think about what happens to you. Your attitudes, values, core philosophies all come under what we term your belief system. In a moment we will show you how your gut feelings are created and sustained by the way you perceive and evaluate (point B) whatever is happening to you at point A.

Where feelings come from

Have you ever wondered what really happens from the moment someone utters some highly critical remarks about your character, say, and the moment you experience a feeling of hurt? First, at the most basic level, the words uttered by the speaker travel through the air as sound waves, impinge upon your ears and are heard as words more or less similar to the words which issued from the speaker's lips. Second, the words must be spoken in a language you recognize and understand. It's no good if the speaker tries to insult you in French if you don't understand a word of it! Next, assuming you understand the actual words, you also have to understand what they really *mean*. This in turn implies a set of shared meanings between speaker and listener within a larger social and cultural context. This explains why jokes don't often register as jokes between people of different social or cultural groups: the degree of shared experience and meaning is missing, even although they might share a common language. Now, let's assume that all those hurdles have been overcome and that you clearly hear and understand exactly what the speaker means when he calls you a slut, for example. Before you can react to the accusation, you appraise it, you evaluate it and *then* you react emotionally. The crucial point here is *how* you react to the speaker's accusation. Do you take it seriously and denigrate yourself? Or do you calmly ignore the imputation and calmly but firmly tell the speaker he is talking drivel and for his own sake had better keep his big mouth shut? The way you interpret and evaluate his remarks will determine how you feel! This is an important lesson to learn: *you feel as you think*.

We're certainly not claiming, however, that it doesn't matter *at all* what is actually happening to us, that, regardless of what happens at point A, we can choose to feel anything we want to feel, as if we are immune to it all. Let's take an example to illustrate this point.

Suppose that you are anxious about failing to pass an exam you have just taken. You know you haven't put in the amount of preparation and study required to pass the exam and you are probably quite correct in predicting that you are going to fail. Now, if you were to fail, and, as a result, you failed to win some advantage, such as being promoted, or qualifying for an additional pay allowance, you could justifiably claim that your exam failure had adversely affected you. And regardless of how you might *feel* about your loss, that loss cannot be denied. So, what happens at A obviously can affect you. And you might also note that A doesn't have to be some external happening in the world; it can be a thought in your head, a prediction that some unwanted occurrence will come about, for example. Just how you feel and react at C to the situation at A will, as we show in RET, be determined largely by B (your belief system) in other words, how you appraise and evaluate what has happened or is likely to happen at A. Thus B causes your emotional and behavioural responses at C, but A contributes to it. If there were no A in your conscious awareness there would be nothing for B to evaluate and work on. And neither at that moment would you experience any particular feeling or reaction at C. So long as you are alive a constant stream of A-type stimuli will pass through your awareness, but relatively few of those stimulus events will be of sufficient interest or importance to you to trigger any emotional response from your nervous system. Which is just as well; life would become virtually impossible if we were to experience strong positive or negative emotions every minute of each waking hour!

Later on, you will learn how your behaviour responds to your thinking and feeling, and in turn influences your thinking and feeling. For the present, we will have made our point if you can accept that there is no way that some event happening far out in the world can, by some magic, get inside your body and cause you in your innermost gut to feel anything. Unless you believe in some kind of voodoo or some other equally superstitious nonsense, there is no way – we repeat, *no way* – any action by anybody can *make* you feel anything, such as humiliated, ashamed or angry, and *force* you to burst into tears or fly into a screaming rage. You are in control of your feelings to a greater degree than you may ever have realized; your emotions are not like a puppet on a string to be jerked up and down at the whim of some external agent over whom you have no control. *You* are in the saddle. Although you are not completely free to choose how you respond emotionally to events in your life – your biological makeup does exert some influence – nevertheless you can learn to think rationally and experience some emotions. We're not aiming in this book to make you less of a feeling person and more of a thinking one. Rational thinking has one main purpose: to increase pleasure and decrease displeasure and pain. We believe that joy, elation and loving are good for us. Reason serves the cause of life, it promotes creativeness and commitment to both short-and long-term goals and aids and abets satisfaction in achievement. Irrationality sabotages joy, and sometimes life itself.

Let's turn our attention now to finding out in more detail how our belief system influences our feelings and behaviour. Our aim will be to show you how to identify the irrational beliefs which you (and practically everybody else) believe in; how and why these beliefs are crazy and inevitably lead to poor results; and how to minimize or eliminate them, and replace them with more realistic, rational convictions. If we succeed in our endeavours, you will have a much better chance of solving your love problems, if and when they arise, without the emotional turmoil which so often surrounds these problems and sabotages the likelihood of a successful outcome.

Why we differentiate rational from irrational beliefs

We call the individual's belief system 'point B' or just 'B'. We can think of B as a collection of core values and beliefs you hold about yourself and the world which make up a framework or set of reference points from which you habitually judge and react to events and experiences happening in the world. Now, you obviously hold a large number of rational, fact-related beliefs about the world you live in. If you didn't you wouldn't live long enough to enjoy it. We are biologically programmed to avoid things which would harm us such as poisonous foods, and to lean towards things which nourish and protect us. As human animals we have the unique capacity to think, to engage in abstract thought, even to think about our thinking. Unfortunately, our brains have no in-built 'fail-safe' device to ensure that our thinking is always a model of clear, accurate perception and logical evaluation of our situation at any time. It may be like that sometimes, but often it isn't! The whole point of trying to distinguish the rational from the irrational components in our thinking is that rational thinking aids and abets human happiness. If we didn't believe that to survive happily in this world and to relate intimately to a few selected others were sensible goals of living we would scarcely bother to encourage and promote rational ways of living, either for ourselves or others. You don't *have* to opt for rational living, of course. You don't *have* to do anything, but we believe that most people would choose happiness as their goal in this life, the only life they know they have.

8

It's important to think and act

Let us assume that you are open-minded enough to try to follow rational dictates of living because you want to see if our teachings can help you to lead a less self-defeating and more self-fulfilling life. But before we begin, a word of warning! What you will read in this book is only the beginning. Merely reading and agreeing with what we write isn't going to do you much good. You may find it all very interesting, but unless you can convince yourself of the truth of what we shall try to teach you, and unless you follow up your reading by *acting* and continuously practising the new patterns of behaviour which will begin to reflect the new more rational philosophy you are trying to acquire, then all the reading in the world will be of little benefit to you.

The RET philosophy we will teach you may *sound* easy, but it isn't! If you want to diet to lose weight, you just eat less. Sounds simple, doesn't it? Just eat less. Cut out this, give up that. What could be simpler? But have you ever met anybody who thinks it's easy? We haven't! It is incredibly difficult to stick rigorously to a weight-loss diet. It demands real determination and loads of self-discipline. You'll find that acquiring the RET philosophy and living by it, immensely rewarding as it is, can be a life-long personal involvement and commitment and that to get the full benefit from it requires lots of hard work and self-discipline. Fortunately, as you proceed through this book, we shall be by your side, so to speak, encouraging you, showing you the way, cajoling you even, to carry out the assignments which we will give you; you may find them a little difficult at first, but they will become easier and even enjoyable with practice.

How to use the A-B-C model to solve your emotional problems: an example of anxiety

As we remarked earlier, many people fail to deal adequately with their love problems, not for want of sensible advice, but because they are too emotionally disturbed to use it. The first step, therefore, in resolving the impasse is to tackle the emotional disturbance first. Until that is out of the way, there is less of a chance that the love problem – whatever it is – will be resolved in a satisfactory manner. The A-B-C model provides you with a framework for conceptualizing the emotional problem and helps you to identify and uproot the irrational components of your belief system which create and sustain your upsetting emotions and self-defeating behaviour. Let's see how the A-B-C model can be used in a problem of anxiety.

Susan and Paul were engaged to be married. Susan worked in the typing pool of a magazine publisher, while Paul was a young advertising executive in the same firm. A colleague of Susan's at work told Susan one morning that she had seen Paul with another girl in a bar the previous evening. They had seemed to be sitting very close, and he had brought her two rounds of drinks while they sat and chatted, apparently oblivious of everyone else in the bar. Susan became anxious. 'What if he's two-timing me?' Susan thought. 'Perhaps it's not the first time; that would be awful! I couldn't stand it if the girls in the pool got to know and began to laugh or feel sorry for me!' A few days passed. Susan spoke to Paul briefly one evening before leaving the office for home, but Paul said nothing about his meeting in the bar. Susan felt that Paul's silence meant that he really was carrying on a secret affair with someone, and she became more anxious. She wrote to an 'agony aunt' about her problem. The advice she received was to 'stay calm, don't jump in with accusations until you know the facts. Tell Paul what you were told about him being seen in the bar and ask him if it is true. If it is true, there might be a perfectly innocent explanation. Give him a chance to explain first.'

That evening, Susan asked Paul over to her flat for dinner. Paul still made no mention of the encounter in the bar and Susan became more and more anxious and more than a little resentful. Paul, noticing that Susan was unusually quiet and withdrawn, suddenly asked: 'What's the matter with *you*?' That did it! 'What's the matter with *me*?' Susan shouted back. 'You secretly see other women behind my back and you ask what's wrong with *me*!' With Susan in tears and refusing to listen to Paul's explanation, Paul walked out and began to have second thoughts about continuing the engagement.

We shall now analyse this episode according to the A-B-C model. We begin with C, the emotional consequence. In Susan's case, it is anxiety. More specifically, it is a form of anxiety called 'ego anxiety'. People suffering from ego anxiety essentially possess a low self-esteem or sense of self-value. They think of themselves in derogatory ways and, because of their negative self-rating, consider themselves unable to cope effectively with what they perceive as threatening situations; that is, situations which they perceive as threatening to their self-esteem. In Susan's case, a poor self-image lies at the heart of her inability to tackle Paul about his alleged affair with another woman. Susan is fearful that if it were true, that would only confirm her low estimation of herself.

At A, the activating event, we have the possibility that Paul is secretly dating another girl. Note that it does not have to be true. The possibility that it *might* be true is what Susan is anxious about. By now, we hope you will have realized that A did not, and cannot cause C. At B, what do you think Susan is telling herself to feel anxiety? Susan has a rational belief: 'I wouldn't like it if Paul really is seeing someone else. There might be nothing in it, of course. He might have bumped into an old friend and decided to have a drink and a chat for old times sake and then forgotten all about it. I can find out by asking him about it the next time we get a chance to talk. If there is really something more to it than that, it puts a question mark over our engagement. Oh well, I'll just have to wait and see what he says.' If Susan stuck with that belief she would feel some concern about the outcome of her confrontation with Paul but not anxious or panicky.

Unfortunately, Susan holds another set of beliefs –irrational beliefs – about the possibility of her fiancée seeing somebody else. 'The threat of Paul leaving me for somebody else is too terrible to contemplate. I don't know how I could deal with it. I'd feel a right fool when the rest of the girls got to hear about it. It just mustn't happen!' Since these irrational beliefs predominate over her more rational beliefs, the resulting feelings are anxiety and panic. Susan was so loath to broach the subject with Paul (for fear that her suspicions would turn out to be well founded) that through her avoidant behaviour she suffered much longer than necessary. It was only when her suspicions were practically forced out of her that she revealed what she was upset about. By that time the damage had been done and all the wise advice she received had been in vain. Sufferers of anxiety tend to avoid or withdraw from the situation they perceive as threatening to their self-esteem in order to obtain relief from the anxiety. That Susan had a poor opinion of herself is clear from her conviction that her friends would think badly of her and that they would be justified in thinking so.

So, what would we do to help Susan dispel her anxiety and tackle her fiancée? First, we would show Susan that her anxiety did not spring from the possibility that her fiancée was dating someone else. There are around one hundred women of Susan's age working in her firm in various departments. Suppose they all were engaged or going steady with someone and then one day discovered that their boyfriends were, each and every one, carrying on with someone else at the same time! Do you think that every single one of those women would become anxious and panicky at the knowledge that their boyfriends were not as exclusively devoted to them as they thought? Highly unlikely! How, then, can it be A which causes your anxiety at C? If you think about it, the real villain is hidden in your belief system (B) – your values, attitudes or philosophies, that you hold about unpleasant activating events or experiences at A. We've already seen the kinds of irrational beliefs Susan held to bring about her crippling anxiety. Now let's show why they are irrational.

Disputing irrational beliefs

Susan tells herself that the possibility of Paul leaving her for somebody else is 'too terrible' to contemplate. But just what do these words really mean? Certainly it cannot be denied that Susan would be inconvenienced and saddened if her fiancée left her for another woman. But does it make any sense to maintain that such a happening is as bad as bad can be? Can you see that such a proposition is quite unverifiable or confirmable by any conceivable appeal to fact? The statement is devoid of any real meaning. It also *demands* that the feared event *should* not, *must* not happen. Granted that it would be annoying and unpleasant for Susan if her fiancée broke off a relationship with Susan which she would rather maintain, where is there a law of God or the universe which says that such things cannot happen? If there were such a law, then obviously, such things *couldn't* happen! But the fact is that such things *do* happen and to maintain that they *must* not happen when they do is to demand that reality *must* not be reality.

In similar vein, Susan believes that she could not possibly cope with the situation if there was a possibility of Paul leaving her. This implies that Susan would fall apart at the seams. But that's hardly likely, is it? What she really means is that she *won't* stand it, and that is really another demand in disguise that it *mustn't* happen. Again, another example of an illogical premise.

Finally, Susan believes that since the other girls will think badly of her, she is a fool or a worthless person. Once more, if Susan were to ask herself how a failure in one aspect of her life *makes* her a fool, she would come up with the answer: 'In no way. Like everyone else, I am a fallible human being with some good traits, some bad. If I fail at one thing, how can that make me a *total* failure? I can work to improve my performances and abilities but I shall never be perfect nor do I need to be. I am me. I accept myself as I am.'

Unconditional self-acceptance is of cardinal importance in acquiring a sane and healthy outlook on life. We shall be returning to this theme again later in this book. For the time being, try to accept that you are not the same thing as your actions, thoughts or behaviours. Humans are an incredibly complex mix of ever-changing traits, acts, deeds, thought and processes. You may rate an individual's abilities or performances in accordance with some standard of measurement, but it is not legitimate to try to rate a human being in terms of some global or overall report card. Our human essence is unmeasurable and essentially unrateable. That is why we caution you against rating your*self* in any way. You can rate how well you play badminton or chess, or play the piano, but you had better not try to rate your personhood.

Concern: the rational alternative to anxiety

We conclude this section by returning briefly to Susan's belief system. We pointed out that Susan held, rather lightly as it turned out, a number of rational beliefs about the possibility of being confronted by a rival for her fiancée's affections. Had she remained with these rational beliefs she would have felt some concern about losing Paul but she would not have felt anxious. It is important to grasp that concern is the rational alternative to anxiety or panic. Study again those beliefs which, if she had held them strongly enough, would have led Susan to feel concern about her situation, rather than anxiety. Why are these beliefs rational? Because they are confirmable by appealing to the facts of the situation. She can prove that she will be inconvenienced if Paul is sharing his time with someone else. She cannot rationally infer anything from Paul's being seen with another girl in a bar other than that he was drinking with and talking to that girl in the bar. Until more information is available, no attributions of motives or intentions are permissible. And Susan could then go on logically to conclude that the sensible thing is to mention the matter to Paul and see what he says. If there should turn out to be a possibility of discussing the termination of the engagement, that, too, could be handled in a sane and sensible manner without tears or hysterics. Anxiety, to sum up what we know so far, is *over*-concern about the possibility of occurrence of some dreaded event in the future, which, if it were to happen, would reveal some personal weakness and thereby imply a loss of self-worth. Feelings of anxiety can be traced back to some variation of the irrational belief that it would be *awful* if such-and-such were to happen, and that you couldn't stand it if it did happen.

You will find the A-B-C model useful for ferreting out the irrational ideas with which you create your anxiety. The model will also help you to question and dispute the irrational ideas behind your anxiety and to replace them with more sensible ones. Later, you will learn how to combine these philosophical methods of combating your irrational beliefs with various techniques to help you depropagandize yourself against anxiety and other forms of emotional disturbance by acting against your irrational notions.

Do not allow anxiety to inhibit you from achieving your individual potential for living life to the full. Wisely avoid obviously hazardous or life-threatening risks if you will, but realize that living inherently involves risk and that a life lived without risk would hardly be worth living.

Other kinds of emotional disturbance

We have dealt at some length with anxiety in the previous pages, using the example of Susan and Paul to illustrate the main points. While space does not permit us to deal with other kinds of emotional problems commonly experienced to quite the same extent as anxiety, we intend now to discuss the other main disturbed emotions which frequently prevent people from satisfactorily solving their love and other relationship problems. These other unhelpful emotions include guilt, anger, depression, shame and embarrassment. In the remainder of this chapter we will confine ourselves to providing an outline of these other emotional problems. We will show you how these problems are generated and sustained by a number of irrational beliefs that people commonly hold, and how, by adopting rational alternative philosophies, these problems can be reduced or eliminated. As we get round to discussing various love problems later in this book, we will again draw your attention to those emotional problems of guilt, anger, and so on, and illustrate in more detail how very unhelpful these disturbed emotions can be to anyone faced with overcoming a love or relationship problem in real life.

Irrational beliefs can take many different forms and be expressed in many different ways. Ellis named twelve irrational ideas which, he maintained, lie at the root of virtually all emotional disturbances. Since these twelve ideas were first enumerated, further study has shown that they can be arranged logically into three groups. We will use these three groups as the basis for our *three main irrational beliefs*, which can be expressed as follows:

(1)   'Because it would be hugely preferable if I were outstandingly competent and/or loved by significant others, I absolutely *should* and *must* be. It is awful when I am not and I am therefore a worthless individual.'

(a)   'Because it is highly desirable that others treat me considerately and fairly, they absolutely *should* and *must* do so and they are rotten people who deserve to be utterly damned when they do not.'

(3)   'Because it is preferable that I experience pleasure rather than pain, the world absolutely *must* arrange this, and life is horrible and I *can't* bear it when the world does not.'

You will find, as you proceed through this book that one or more of these three main irrational beliefs underlie and maintain anxiety and all the other disturbed emotions we are about to discuss. They are the main factors underlying virtually all neurosis and character disorder. In other words, the essence of just about all human disturbance is

14

demandingness. Now that you've seen how anxiety and worry are created by unnecessary and exaggerated fears about something that might happen, let us now go on to look at one of the most self-defeating emotional disturbances human beings can plague themselves with: guilt.

Guilt

Guilt feelings spring from the belief that you have broken some personal code of morals or rule of personal behaviour. This may take the form of an act of commission ('I have done something wrong') or omission ('I failed to do what I thought was right').

The irrational ideas behind guilt

It is important to realize that the inferences noted above do not of themselves create a feeling of guilt. Guilt arises when a person believes: 'I absolutely *should not* have done what I did, or I absolutely *should* have done what I failed to do. I am, therefore, a damnable individual for doing what I did, or failed to do, and deserve to be punished.'

You have already seen in our treatment of anxiety why expressions involving 'should' and 'must' in the absolute sense are simply grandiose demands that the world must be different than it is, and are therefore highly irrational.

Behavioural reactions to guilt feelings

Actions that people may take to 'atone' for their guilt often do little to improve the situation and instead make the situation even worse. Here are some typical responses:

(1)   A conviction that one must punish oneself in some fitting way, for example by inflicting physical harm on oneself.
(2)   Desperately begging forgiveness from someone assumed to have been wronged by one's action, and usually accompanied by an acute sense of self-loathing. Even the most abject apologies usually fail to assuage the intense feeling of self-hatred which accompanies such behaviour.
(3)   Attempting to escape from the torment of guilt by over-indulgence in alcohol or drugs.
(4)   Denial of responsibility or defensive excuses aimed at shifting the blame on to someone else in order to escape the pain of guilt.

Note that self-condemnation is a characteristic accompaniment of these reactions and does little if anything to improve the situation or help the guilty person to take appropriate action to put right whatever wrong was committed in the first place.

Remorse: the rational alternative to guilt

The rational alternative to guilt is remorse. The inferences are the same as in guilt; the crucial difference lies in the beliefs the person holds about the wrongs committed. In remorse, a person adopting a rational view of the situation would be convinced of something like: 'I admit I did the wrong thing, or failed to do the right thing. I don't like what I did, but there's no reason why I *must* not have done it. I am a fallible human being who did the wrong thing but I am not damnable for it.'

A person who adopts this position from genuine conviction has a much better chance of accepting responsibility for having acted badly and of being motivated to make appropriate restitution without in any way humbling himself or being unduly apologetic. It is important to realize that *being* guilty of a misdemeanour simply means that you accept responsibility for your action. That is not the same thing as *feeling* guilty, that is, condemning yourself as a person for having carried out the actions. The difference lies in the beliefs you hold about your behaviour. Rational beliefs will lead you to feel remorse, irrational beliefs will hogtie you with guilt. When we come to dealing with problems of love and relationships you will appreciate how important our distinction is between guilt and remorse.

Depression

The main inferences made by a person in a depressed state are that the person has suffered a significant loss of a personal kind. This might be the death of some significant other, the loss of a limb or some form of personal functioning, or it might be, and often is, the loss of a valued love relationship. It can also be the loss associated with failure to achieve a valued goal, such as achieving concert status as a violin player or earning enough money to secure a comfortable retirement.

As you may now realize, it is not the inferences of personal loss *per se* which cause depression but the particular irrational beliefs the individual holds about his or her loss. Typically, the depressed person believes: 'I absolutely should not have experienced this loss. It is terrible, and I can't stand it.' Depending on the nature of the loss, the individual concludes 'I am no good' or that 'the world is a rotten place for allowing the loss to occur, poor me'. When these irrational beliefs are firmly entrenched, it is little wonder that depressed people often feel hopeless about the future. If you remember the three main irrational beliefs, you should experience no difficulty in identifying at least one of these beliefs in the genesis of depression as described above.

16

Behavioural reactions to depression

Withdrawal from previously enjoyed activities and from valued friends is typical in depression. The depressed person is often inert, unsociable, and may attempt to 'drown' the depression by resorting to alcohol or drugs in order to escape the pain of depression. You will also frequently observe a loss of self-discipline and a conviction that nothing can be done to improve the situation (a combination of hopelessness and helplessness).

Sadness: the rational alternative to depression

Here, the person makes the same inferences about having experienced a personal loss as in depression, but her beliefs about the loss are rational – that is, they are realistic and lead to constructive action. 'It's bad that this loss has occurred but it isn't terrible. There is no reason why it shouldn't have happened. I'll survive and perhaps in time I'll be able to do something to make up for my loss.' The sad person is able to talk about his or her loss with friends and associates and is able to avoid withdrawal into herself as occurs in depression.

Anger

You may be forgiven for wondering why we include anger as an emotional problem to be avoided. A cleric recently said on TV that it is right to feel angry. He called it 'righteous anger'. Well, whether anger is 'righteous' or not we doubt if its consequences are beneficial to either the person who is angry or to the person on the receiving end of the anger. We could make a good case for the proposition that anger is responsible for the break-up of relationships more than any other single factor. Perhaps for that reason alone you may think it time well spent in looking at the causes and the consequences of anger.

In anger one typically says that a frustrating event or circumstance has occurred or exists which blocks one from achieving a valued personal goal. Or it may be that some person or institution has transgressed some personal rule deemed important in one's personal domain. A third type of anger arises after one makes an inference that the actions of some other person or institution threaten one's 'self-esteem'.

By now you may be expecting to find some set of beliefs which involve damning of other people, the world or even oneself. Reduced to basics, the angry person believes: 'You must not act in this way and you are damnable for doing so.' Once more, observe that 'must not'! If the source of frustration lies within oneself, the angry person damns himself or herself.

A form of anger which commonly occurs in love relationships which have gone a bit rocky is 'ego-defensive anger'. Here, the anger is used as a cover-up for a low sense of self-esteem. It may also serve as a cover-up for anxiety (for example, anxiety over the possible loss of some valued person's love). The anger serves to direct attention away from the person's low level of self-esteem.

It will be useful to spell out the irrational beliefs behind ego-defensive anger. As an example, consider the case of a man who is angry with his girlfriend for criticizing him for what he sees as a personal inadequacy. If the man holds a low view of himself he will not only feel hurt by the criticism but also anxious at the implication that she may no longer care to continue their relationship – and that would be *terrible*! Since he feels that such an outcome would be the end of all his most cherished wishes for happiness, such an outcome *must not* happen! The anger therefore serves as a rebuke to the woman for not caring for him as much as she should, for ignoring all that he had done for her, and so on.

Another example may be seen in the woman who is angry with her husband for failing to bring her a card and flowers on her birthday. In her view, not only has her husband broken a rule of behaviour which she deems important, but his neglect or forgetfulness is inferred as evidence of an uncaring attitude or even loss of love on his part. This inference that he has acted uncaringly towards her is followed by the belief that it is terrible to be treated this way, and that she did not deserve it. The consequent feeling is one of hurt, while her anger covers up the feeling of hurt which she may be afraid to reveal in case it is seen by her husband as a personal weakness.

Behavioural responses to anger

A common response to anger is verbal or physical aggression, or both. The person on the receiving end may be cowed, at least temporarily, into submission, and may withdraw from the angry one. Or, as frequently happens, aggression invites retaliation, with potentially serious consequences. The damage done to a close personal relationship can be immense, often irreparable. Apart from its effects on relationships, anger can cause high blood pressure or cardio-vascular disorders. The use of anger can scarcely be recommended, despite what some clerics and politicians may claim. There is, of course, a rational alternative to anger, and it is important to understand this.

Annoyance: the rational alternative to anger

Again, the inferences are the same as in anger, but the beliefs about the frustrations, rule transgressions or whatever are rational: 'I don't like your behaviour and I wish you didn't act in this way. But there's no reason why you should not, or must not, act in this bad manner. You are not damnable for it, but merely a fallible human being who is, in my view, acting badly.' Acceptance of the other person as a fallible human being is an important aspect of annoyance and it is important that you remember this.

The alternative to that form of anger we term 'ego-defensive' for reasons which we hope are now clear to you, is again annoyance. Since ego-defensive anger derives from a basic lack of self-acceptance or self-esteem, the obvious way to tackle the problem is to highlight those irrational beliefs which lead to a low level of self-acceptance and then proceed to show why these beliefs are untenable. Once these irrational beliefs are cleared away and replaced by more rational and realistic convictions, the individual can become truly self-accepting and thus able to handle criticisms of personal inadequacy without feeling hurt by them or induced to seeing himself or herself as a worthless person. As a fallible human being you can accept yourself with your failings or inadequacies without damning yourself for having them. And the more self-accepting you become, the more accepting of others you will become and the less prone will you be to damning them for their actions. Thus, when you are criticized for some failing or personal inadequacy you can rationally convince yourself: 'Yes, I acted badly and I feel annoyed at my poor behaviour but I'm not a rotten person for exhibiting my poor behaviour. Now, let me see how I can figure out a way of correcting these failings and acting more consistently in an adequate and appropriate manner in future.'

When your annoyance is directed at someone else over some breach of behaviour, say, it is useful to remember that annoyance or intense displeasure tends to encourage you to remain in the situation and that it is better to try and figure out some constructive response for dealing with the situation; this could mean assertively requesting (not demanding!) a change of behaviour on the part of the other person. The important point here is that in annoyance, you tend to view the situation as a problem to be solved, rather than some life or death issue to be fought over. The importance of this for dealing with love problems is obvious.

Shame and embarrassment

Although perhaps not so much of a disadvantage in dealing with love and relationships as anger, guilt and other kinds of emotional upset, a few words about the causes of shame and embarrassment may not be out of place.

The inferences made in shame are that the person has revealed a personal weakness or has acted stupidly in public, and that others will notice this display and take a negative view of the person for so behaving. In embarrassment, the same types of inference are made, except that the personal weakness or social gaffe is regarded as less serious than in shame.

The irrational beliefs behind shame and embarrassment

The person displaying the weakness tends to believe: 'They're right, I am worthless for revealing my weakness.' This negative self-evaluation stems from the belief: 'I must not reveal my weakness in public' and 'I must not be disapproved of by other people'. Thus, the negative evaluation of oneself and the irrational beliefs which generate and sustain it are at the core of shame and embarrassment. Typical behavioural reactions are withdrawal from the situation and from others who may have witnessed the personal weakness, and blushing. In extreme cases a feeling of panic or being trapped may be experienced.

Regret: the rational alternative to shame and embarrassment

In regret, the inferences are again the same but the beliefs about displaying the weakness and the inferred negative evaluation by others are rational: 'I don't like the fact that I acted stupidly in public and that people who saw me may think badly of me. That's too bad. But there's no reason why I must not have committed this blunder in public or that others must not think badly of me. It's too bad, but it's not terrible, and I can still choose to accept myself as a fallible human being for acting in this way.' Holding this view of the situation gives the person room to restore the situation, without the need for complete withdrawal. He or she may focus on the funny side of it if there is one, or make a dignified apology if that is called for. It may also be possible to enlist the help of others to restore the social equilibrium with the minimum of fuss.

Summary

(1) Realize that you (and no one else) create your emotional feelings (C).

(2) No matter how badly others behave or treat you at point A, it is your beliefs about their behaviour which upset you at point C. Although events at A contribute to your feelings, they do not cause them.

(3) Every time you feel seriously upset you are holding both a rational and an irrational belief. Rationally, you say to yourself: 'I don't like this! It's too bad that it exists. I wish very much I could change it!' Irrationally you say: 'How awful that this exists or has

happened! I can't stand it! It shouldn't be! I'm a bad person for allowing it to exist!'

(4)   If you dispute your irrational beliefs until you can see the absurdity of them, they will tend to diminish and even disappear. Your aim is to arrive at a fundamentally different non-demanding philosophy of life that will make it difficult for you to upset yourself over virtually any unfortunate thing that may happen to you.

(5)   We find it easy to upset ourselves, partly through our upbringing and environmental influences, and partly through our biological disposition to bigotedly believe that we *need* what we want, and that we *must* have it, and it is awful when we are deprived of it.

(6)   Provided that you work at and practise finding and disputing your irrational notions you will lay the groundwork for a rational, more satisfying view of life with benefits to your loved ones as well.

2

'A Good Man Is Hard to Find'

How true this is! However, before we go any further, we had better say what we mean by 'a good man'. There are several aspects to the word 'good'. First, it doesn't stand by itself. Whenever we see the word 'good', a question arises in our minds: 'good' for whom? Or 'good' for what? If something is good, it must be good *for* some person or some purpose. It follows that, from your point of view, a 'good' man is a man who is 'good for me'; not one who your mother, or father or girlfriend thinks is good for you, but one who you decide is good for *you* – someone you feel you can trust; someone you feel comfortable with; someone who shares your deepest values; someone who treats you the way you want to be treated. Later on in this book we'll offer you some suggestions about the qualities of mind and character you might like to consider if you are looking for a long-term relationship with a member of the opposite sex. Not that you have to have a relationship with a man! Some women prefer their own company; they're quite happy to live without a man in their lives. Or you might love domestic animals and want nothing more than to spend your life looking after them. Others again may prefer the company of other women and may enjoy, and intend to maintain, an ongoing intimate relationship with some similarly inclined partner of the same sex. If that is your particular cup of tea, fine. It is no part of our brief to try to change your preferences. It seems, however, that the majority of women prefer to have a man in their lives, and while we obviously write with their interests in mind, this by no means excludes those of you who hold different ideas. Almost anybody can experience emotional difficulties in their personal relationships, regardless of their sexual orientation or lifestyle. Whether or not you have a man in your life and whether or not you want one, you may find that what we have to say in this book can help you, perhaps in unexpected ways, to get on better with those people or partners you do choose to live with on an intimate basis.

Now, let's return to this question of what is 'a good man'. If you return to Chapter 1 and reread what we said about rating yourself, you will see that our remarks about giving oneself a global rating are relevant to what we are discussing here. While you may legitimately rate your acts as good or bad, you cannot logically rate your entire self as good or bad; indeed, you cannot measure it in any way. In other words, when you act well, that doesn't make you a good person, because a 'good person' is someone who is wholly good and cannot be anything else but good. Similarly, if you rate yourself as a bad person on the basis of having committed misdeeds, or having acted badly or unethically, you are making the same mistake: evaluating your entire self or being on the basis of your actions. The point is, very simply, that *you* are not the same thing as *your traits or behaviour*. Can you see now that describing someone as a good person, or as a bad person, really amounts to giving that person a global rating?

Which brings us back to what we pointed out at the beginning of this chapter: a good man means 'good for me'. So, what might you be looking for if you are in the market for a man with whom you could seriously contemplate having a close, long-term relationship? Let us now take a look at some important considerations involved in finding a suitable partner, and also at some of the pitfalls to be avoided.

Obstacles to finding a 'good' man

There are two main categories of obstacle confronting you, at least potentially. You are unlikely to meet them all although you could be unlucky and find yourself faced with them at some time or other.

Category 1: Social or societal obstacles

The first category consists of obstacles created by the particular society you were born and reared in. These comprise:

Geographical obstacles

If you live in a small village remote from larger centres of population, and your mobility is restricted, you may find that the number of potential partners for you is too limited, thus placing too tight a restriction on your choice.

Social obstacles

Every society has its rules and customs governing what you should and shouldn't do. Not all of them are necessarily enforced by law, but even those that are not legally binding still exercise a considerable influence upon individuals to 'toe the line' as far as conduct with the opposite sex is concerned. You may think that some of these social mores are outdated, a legacy perhaps of the male-dominated past when women had far less freedom and equality of opportunity than they have today, but they can still prove irksome, even in today's partially improved climate, to modern, independent-minded women who know what they want and have scant regard for the cobwebbed rules of behaviour their mothers and grandmothers lived by and took for granted.

Cultural obstacles

You may find yourself faced with restrictions imposed by your culture. One of these is 'you mustn't marry outside the faith'. This restriction is not necessarily a foolish one. You might easily be attracted to someone with a different religion or with no religion at all, but a clash of values is then possible, especially if you marry and decide to bring up children. Having said that, we are aware that happy marriages have taken place between individuals of different faiths or religious backgrounds. In general, however, we would not recommend forming an intimate partnership with someone with *fundamentally* different religious convictions to your own, *if* you both take your religion seriously. Having a common religion doesn't necessarily lead to a harmonious relationship, of course, but two different religions with conflicting values have plenty of potential for causing problems in any relationship.

Category 2: Emotional problems

Unlike the first category of obstacles, many of which were in existence before you were born and are relatively resistant to change, the obstacles in this category are mainly the self-created emotional disturbances we met in Chapter 1. In the next section we will take a closer look at one of them – anxiety.

Anxiety

As we discussed in Chapter 1, anxiety is really *over*-concern about some possible future happening or outcome. How does anxiety prevent you from going after what you want or make you less effective in achieving your goal than you would be without the anxiety? It can manifest itself in one of two ways, which will cause you either to try too hard or not to try at all.

There is a world of difference between *preferring* a man in your life and *needing* one. Some women are unsuccessful in finding the kind of man they want because they try too hard. Here is why desperately looking for a man won't help you find a suitable one.

As soon as you convince yourself that you absolutely *must* have something – such as the love or esteem of some man you've met, and that you couldn't possibly be happy without him, you will tend to do all the wrong things to achieve your objective. Why? Because you will feel so anxious, so over-concerned about the possibility of *not* getting what you so desperately think you *must* have, that you will tend to act in foolish and exaggerated ways instead of calmly using whatever social skills and natural charm you may have to attract the attention of the individual whose attributes you admire so much. You will be so anxious about making a good impression upon this individual that your spontaneity and ease of manner with him will be inhibited by your fear of saying the wrong thing or giving him the impression that you are not too bright, or even appearing a little naive. You saw in Chapter 1 how Susan's anxiety over losing her fiancée to another woman led her into an emotional turmoil which not only caused her pain and unhappiness, but nearly precipitated the break-up of her engagement.

But anxiety can also cause you not to take any action at all to win the esteem or interest of some man who really appeals to you. This may happen if you have already lost out with some man you very much wanted to get close to because of some mistakes you made in the early stages of your relationship. The thought that you might fail again with this new man, and how awful that would be, freezes you into immobility. 'How awful it would be if I screwed up this chance! I couldn't go through that period of misery again.' This is what you tell yourself, and rather than risk yet another failure, you do nothing, and let the chance of winning this man pass you by. Perhaps you eventually settle for some ordinary fellow who doesn't exactly inspire you but whom you know you can easily attract, telling yourself that half a loaf is better than no bread. That may be true in some areas of life, but sadly, it doesn't apply in the game of love. 'Alright, it would be very nice if I could meet some attractive guy and feel at ease while we got to know each other, but how do I avoid feeling a bit anxious when I meet some really outstanding man?' you might ask. Well, for a start, you need to become aware of how anxiety is created.

How we talk ourselves into feeling anxious

If you really decide to go for what you really want in an intimate long-term relationship with a man, how can you overcome your anxiety, or, better still, not feel anxious at all? The answer is to tackle your underlying insecurity. You will find it helpful to use the A-B-C model of emotional disturbance which we described in Chapter 1. This provides you with a framework with which you can visualize how your anxiety (or any other disturbing emotion) is created and what you can do to eliminate it. Before we go into detail, let's set the scene by looking at a typical problem experienced by some women.

Linda, an attractive 30-year-old advertising executive, met Geoff at a party. Of all the men present at that party, Geoff was the one who attracted her the most. He was good-looking, charming, amusing and considerate. She and Geoff got on together just great. Linda was over the moon when, as the party drew to a close, Geoff asked her for a date one evening the following week. For several days before the date of their meeting, Linda was looking forward to the event with eager anticipation. Perhaps he would turn out to be the man she had been looking for over the past few years but had yet to find! True, Linda had had a few boyfriends and had high hopes of at least two of them resulting in the kind of close, loving, long-term relationship she really wanted, but somehow it didn't happen. After a short spell of dating, Linda's hopes would be dashed as the men lost interest and drifted away. And to make matters worse, Linda's mother was dropping remarks more and more often to the effect that it was time her daughter was thinking of settling down like so many other of Linda's friends had done by the time they had reached Linda's age. 'It was all too much!' thought Linda. 'Here I am trying my hardest to find the right guy, while my mother carries on about how I'm wasting the best years of my life just playing around! Well, this time I'll show her!'

As the big day drew near, Linda's feelings of eager anticipation changed to feelings of increasing anxiety. All sorts of thoughts began to bother her. It was great at the party with plenty of drink and dancing to that fabulous music, but what would it be like in the different surroundings of that top restaurant where Geoff was taking her to dinner? What should she wear? Would it be the 'right' thing? And what would they talk about? Would Geoff, perish the thought, find her boring or uninteresting like one or two of her previous boyfriends had sort of hinted? The more 'what-ifs' Linda kept bringing up, the more anxious she felt. She even toyed with the idea of calling off the whole thing on some pretext or other. But then she felt even more anxious at the thought that she could be throwing away the chance of a lifetime if she called the date off and she never saw Geoff again. So Linda had the worst of it on both counts; she felt anxious about keeping her date with Geoff and anxious about calling it off.

We hope it is clear to you by now that it isn't the situation Linda finds herself in that makes her feel anxious. It is what she is telling herself about the situation that creates her anxiety. If Linda wants to feel differently about her forthcoming encounter with Geoff, then she will have to think differently about it. Now, we are certainly not claiming that whenever you feel pain or discomfort, you can just think it out of existence. Pain is real, and you scarcely need us to tell you that. What we are saying is that if you feel anxious or depressed about some event or possible happening in your life, and there is no obvious physical or medical reason for your discomfort, then the chances are that it arises from the manner in which you are thinking about your situation. There may well be a real problem or difficulty confronting you, but you will find that the way you appraise and evaluate the problem can make a difference to whether or not you obtain a satisfactory outcome. In other words, if you have an emotional problem such as anxiety, depression or anger at point C, then the situation or event at point A which contributes to your emotional problem will be more difficult to resolve than if you avoided the emotional problem in the first place. A good rule of thumb to remember when you find yourself in some kind of emotional difficulty over how to handle a real life problem is: 'You largely feel as you think'. It follows that if you want to feel differently about some event in your life, then you have to think differently about it. Let's return now to Linda and find out how she came to dread an encounter she had been eagerly anticipating, and see what she could do to overcome her anxiety.

The irrational beliefs which create anxiety

Put yourself in Linda's place and suppose that, like Linda, you felt anxious at the prospect of your impending date with Geoff being not only the first one, but the last. What kinds of irrational belief would you expect to find buzzing around in your head? We suspect you would be telling yourself: 'I must, absolutely *must*, make a hit with Geoff on our first date and if I don't, that will be terrible! It would prove there is something radically wrong with me and that I'm probably never going to be worthy of winning any really good man no matter how long I keep trying.' Can you see why these beliefs are quite irrational, unprovable and in no way supported by any factual evidence? Think it through. Ask yourself how anyone could ever prove that a failure to live up to your expectations on a date means that failure will *always* result and that this in turn implies that you are no good at all. Can you see that if Linda demands (not merely prefers) that something must, or must not, happen, and that her worth as a human being depends upon the outcome, then anxiety is practically inevitable? Linda didn't only believe that it would be disappointing and unfortunate if she failed to relate well on her date. That belief would be rational because Linda could honestly say that she really would be disappointed and saddened if something she wanted to come about failed to do so. We would all feel disappointed if a much prized opportunity to reach some goal were to turn out badly. Where Linda came unstuck was her irrational demand that she *had* to succeed with Geoff and that she would be an utter failure as a person if she didn't. In effect, Linda was risking her entire worth as a human being, risking her respect for herself, on the possibility of not coming over well on her date with Geoff and therefore probably not seeing him again. With so much at stake, could Linda have been anything else but extremely anxious?

Although we discussed this in Chapter 1, we want to reiterate here that the rational alternative to anxiety is concern. If something is important to you, such as making a good first impression on a date or on a job interview, it would be wise to be concerned about doing your best and how to go about it. There is no sense in pretending to yourself that the outcome doesn't matter, because you know that it does. The rational alternative to feeling panicky about the outcome of some future event that means a lot to you is not to adopt a devil-may-care attitude; rather, the rational response consists of convincing yourself that yes, it is important for you to do well on this special occasion, but it isn't all important, it isn't a matter of life and death. You believe you can succeed if you do your best. There is no reason why you can't actually enjoy this challenge, so go in there and let yourself do just that. And if you fail, well that's tough, but that's all it is. You may have failed on this occasion but there's always the next – and the next!

But how do you actually change your feelings of anxiety to feelings of concern? Will just strengthening your rational responses do the trick? You have to be convinced deep down inside you that these rational beliefs can be upheld and that they work. And *that* requires time as well as work and practice. We will show you presently how you can strengthen your anti-anxiety convictions by acting against, as well as disputing, your anxiety-creating thoughts and beliefs. As with other forms of emotional disturbance, identifying and changing the irrational beliefs which create and sustain them is an important step, an essential step in fact, but it is only a first step.

How to strengthen your rational beliefs

We have stated that giving your intellectual assent to rational beliefs is fine, but that by itself this will usually be insufficient to substantially reduce your level of anxiety (or any other emotional difficulty). Throughout this book we will try to teach you several ways of combating irrational ideas and attitudes which can seriously interfere with initiating or maintaining a good relationship with someone special. In the following paragraphs we show you how you can begin to tackle your anxiety about failing to make a good impression on someone important. It is a good idea to get into the habit of using these techniques until they become second nature.

First, practise disputing your irrational beliefs. Devote ten minutes each day to identifying and disputing the irrational beliefs which we showed you are the main culprits in creating and sustaining your feelings of anxiety. Go over them until you see that they really make no sense, that they are illogical and inconsistent with reality, and that you will continue to get poor results as long as you continue to believe them.

Next, study the rational alternative beliefs. Spend another ten minutes each day thinking through the rational beliefs we presented you with and try rephrasing them in your own words so that they are relevant to you. Convince yourself that your rational beliefs can stand up to critical examination. If you can, persuade a friend to play the devil's advocate by arguing against your rational beliefs to give you practice in demolishing the opposite point of view and thereby deepen and strengthen your rational convictions.

Having thought about them, you must then *act* against your irrational beliefs. Unless you repeatedly act against some habitual or deep-rooted irrational fear, you will rarely eliminate it. If, for example, you are anxious about accepting a date with someone in case you are turned down and you avoid accepting the invitation in order to escape the 'horror' of being found unacceptable, you unconsciously reinforce your anxiety. By running away from the situation, you are clearly telling yourself, even if you are not aware of it: 'It would be *awful* if I were rejected! I couldn't stand that so I must be *sure* I'll be accepted before I risk going on another date.' And, if you do force yourself to accept the date while still believing that you *must* succeed and that it would be quite dreadful if you didn't, you will be so tensed up and uncomfortable while you are in the other person's company, that you will probably convey a disappointing impression to your partner who will think he has been mistaken about you and that there would be no point in seeing you again. So you lose confidence and become even more afraid.

The antidote is to tackle your irrational anxiety-creating beliefs forcefully and often, and as you weaken them and replace them with more rational beliefs, *act* against your anxious tendencies (they will still be there, albeit in a less intense form) by initiating friendly overtures with men you find attractive, accepting dates with them in spite of your horror of rejection, and continuing to do so until you see that nothing 'horrible' happens even when some of your dates get no further than the first. By persisting with this double-barrelled attack on your anxiety-creating ideas you will weaken them to the point where they will rarely trouble you. Then, as a consequence of your more relaxed attitude, you will enjoy your dates, you will allow your natural charm and spontaneity full rein, and, who knows, you may even find men beating a path to your door for the pleasure of taking you out!

Now put yourself in Linda's shoes once again, but this time imagine you have made good progress in overcoming your previously inhibiting anxiety by using the anxiety-combating methods outlined above. You are looking forward with anticipation to your date with Geoff which you hope will be the start of a relationship with him. Now what would you, given your position, be telling yourself about the possibility of the meeting with Geoff not working out as well as you hope it does? Remember, you want very much to get into a long-term involvement with this man, who strikes you as really outstanding. If you were thinking rationally, your response would be along the lines of: 'I would very much like to make a good impression on Geoff so that he would like to continue seeing me. He is a very attractive man and I believe we could have a very good relationship together. But if it doesn't work out that way, that would be disappointing and very unfortunate but not the end of the world.' As a consequence of telling yourself that it would be disappointing and very unfortunate for you if nothing came of your date, how do you think you would feel? Doubtless you would feel very sad about it. It would be too bad if your high hopes failed to materialize. You could quite justifiably argue that you will lose out on a lot of life's pleasures and future happiness if you don't relate well to the men you meet. But that doesn't mean that you could never be happy under *any* circumstances! It just means that you might not be as happy as you could be if you were to succeed in winning the relationship you have set your sights on. In fact, your sorrow at not relating well enough with men could provide you with the determination to work very hard to rid yourself of this annoying condition simply because you do want to relate well and are bothered by the fact that you haven't so far. In short, your rational response to the possibility of your date falling through would enable you to feel concerned if it were to happen but not overcome with anxiety. And your disappointment at your failure to relate well could motivate you to get your act together so that you do much better in that respect with any future man you might meet.

'*I always seem to pick the wrong man*'

In our personal experience – and perhaps in yours as well – many men and women, having ended a marriage or a long period of living together, eventually wind up marrying or getting deeply involved emotionally with another person with remarkably similar behavioural characteristics and even looks to the former partner. Psychoanalytically inclined writers have penned books on the subject, purporting to explain how these 'same-again' relationships are caused by some deep unconscious desire to achieve union with some father or mother figure which was thwarted in the childhood past. Imaginative and fascinating though some of these accounts undoubtedly are, it is not our intention to burden you with far-fetched theories as to how your propensity to choose unsuitable partners may have originated. Instead, we hope to go more directly to the root of the problem (if it should be a problem) by offering helpful suggestions to enable you to avoid picking an unsuitable partner in the first place, or of repeating the mistake in the second place.

There are, of course, several reasons why you might be attracted initially to someone who is quite unsuitable for you. If you have not had much experience of meeting and going out with men, you might be charmed by a particular style of behaviour or seduced into believing a particular line of chat delivered with wit and panache. However, even if you have learned, as we hope you have, quite a bit about the ways and wiles of the opposite sex, you could still find it easy to get involved with someone who seems good for you but who sooner or later turns out to have been a waste of your time. How does this come about? Well, when one is serious about finding a partner to get involved with on a long-term basis, there is a temptation to save time by taking shortcuts. Even if you accept yourself and play the dating and mating game without experiencing anxiety when you fail to relate well, or without feeling hostility towards a man for not appreciating your good qualities when he leaves you for someone who isn't even in the same league as you in terms of brains and looks, you can still ruin things if you subscribe to the third main irrational belief introduced in Chapter 1: 'Because it is preferable that I experience pleasure rather than pain, the world absolutely must arrange this, and life is horrible and I can't bear it when the world does not.'

This is an example of low frustration tolerance (or LFT). There are several variants of this irrational belief and the others listed in Chapter 1. These beliefs are widely held because they are part of our culture. They are propounded in some form or other in stories, plays, films and music. That is not the only reason why we believe them. Because we are human, we find it easy to think in absolutistic ways. Slightly misquoting Voltaire: 'If our culture did not propound irrational ideas to us, we would easily invent them ourselves.'

In the present context, LFT may well be re-expressed as 'I shouldn't have to try so hard to get what I want, even though I know I will benefit in the long run by trying hard. It's *too* hard to put in so much effort for my own happiness. I need immediate gratification.'

Let's see how the demand for comfort – this demand that you shouldn't have to put in so much effort to find a suitable partner – can lead to a woman complaining: 'I always seem to pick the wrong man.' First, we tend to feel comfortable with what is familiar to us. This can apply to a person or a situation even though the person or situation may be far from satisfactory in many other respects. Making a change from the familiar to the unfamiliar, such as moving house, changing your job, or looking for a new love partner, can be a source of inconvenience and therefore of some degree of discomfort.

Now, if you have left a relationship with someone and are starting to look for someone new, you are unlikely to find someone who is right for you on your very first date. Nor are you likely to meet the kind of man you want unless you widen your range and give yourself a chance to meet a variety of men with backgrounds rather different to those you may have been content to restrict yourself to in the past. But this means taking risks with the unfamiliar! It may mean changing your dating pattern, going to unfamiliar places, giving up, at least temporarily, some of your old and familiar haunts and finding yourself in places and situations you are not conversant with. If you hold the irrational belief that you *must* be comfortable with your dating pattern and that putting yourself out to make real changes, rather than mere cosmetic changes, is *too* much trouble and it *shouldn't* be so hard, you will tend to take the easy way out and stick to your old haunts. The trouble is that this so-called 'easy' way is only easy for you in the short run. By continuing to go along to that regular church group meeting or to that social club where you met your previous men friends, you will no doubt meet the type of man you are familiar with, but who could well turn out to be the type that your previous experience tells you is bad for you! So how do you avoid repeating your previous mistakes and give yourself a fair chance to meet the kind of partner with whom you could have a better relationship? Answer: by disputing the irrational beliefs which underlie your LFT and replacing them with more helpful rational convictions.

Irrational ideas which create low frustration tolerance

A variant of the third main irrational belief we met in Chapter 1, which applies more specifically to the problem of always picking the wrong man may be expressed thus: 'If I break with my old pattern of dating and begin to look for suitable men in unfamiliar surroundings I may bring about more acute discomfort, and since I couldn't stand feeling that way I will not risk changing. My previous partner seemed to be OK but he wasn't. I was just unlucky and since I've met other men in his social group who seem to be OK, I'm sure that one of them will be OK. I want my future to be a happy one, but I shouldn't have to try so hard to achieve it. Besides, it's *too* hard to change my whole way of meeting new potential partners, and I don't see why I should make life so hard for myself. Not everybody has to go to such trouble to win a good man, so why should I? My life *must* be easy and conditions *must* be arranged so that I get exactly what I want in a reasonable time, and it's unbearable if I don't.'

Now look for the evidence behind that statement. Is there any? If life *must* be easy, if there were some law of the universe which decreed that life for human beings must be easy and that they must get what they want without having to wait too long for it, wouldn't it be so? You know that life is *not* like that. So, does it make any sense to demand that what obviously does not exist *must* exist? Like it or not, there are no guarantees in this life.

What does it mean to claim that it is 'too hard' to go to the trouble of making a fresh start by visiting new and unfamiliar places to meet new men? Is it impossible? No. Is it uncomfortable at first? Possibly. It might even be quite hard to break established habits and move comfortably in new social circles. But how can it be *too* hard? If something is possible, it may be easy to accomplish, or it may present moderate to great difficulty. But where on the scale of difficulty is the mark 'too hard'? Nowhere, except in your head!

You claim that you couldn't stand the discomfort of looking in unfamiliar venues for new men friends. Does that mean you would come apart at the seams if you tried it? Surely not! And as for your prediction that because some fella *seems* OK, therefore he *will* be OK, isn't that rather a rash statement, especially in view of your previous sad experience? Do you have any real grounds for believing that the next time will be any better? Or is it not simply a case of wishful thinking derived from your discomfort anxiety at the thought of getting completely away from your old, relatively comfortable, ways of meeting men and starting out anew without the certainty that next time you will succeed?

Some rational answers to low frustration tolerance

If you now see, as we hope you do, that the beliefs we discussed above are irrational because they are unrealistic, illogical and more likely to hinder than to help you to achieve your goals, what rational beliefs could you substitute for the irrational ones to give you a better chance of finding the right man for you? We suggest the following rational answers would be worth thinking through:

If you break with your old pattern of dating and begin to look for suitable men in less familiar surroundings than those you've been used to, you may well experience discomfort but you can stand it. There is no reason why doing something a little differently should feel comfortable right from the start. In fact, just because it is new or different you can expect it to feel strange at first. So there is no reason not to risk changing. And in view of the poor results your previous dating pattern produced, maybe you'd better change it.

Just because a man *seems* to be OK, that doesn't mean he is, or will be, OK. By making such an unwarranted assumption you are giving yourself an excuse in advance to avoid doing any real searching to find out what kind of man he really is because to do so would take time and effort and expose you to the risk of failure, and that would feel uncomfortable. But it is better to face a little possible discomfort now than have to live with much greater discomfort later as a consequence of taking the easy option and committing yourself to a man who at first sight seems OK.

Of course, you want a happy future, but there is no reason why you absolutely must get it or that you shouldn't have to work hard to achieve your goals. If it's hard, it's hard, and if you truly want what you want as much as you think you do you had better uncomplainingly do whatever you know you have to do to achieve it. No pain, no gain. So if changing your whole way of meeting potential partners is difficult then so be it, but you'd best put up with the difficulty now in order to meet a bigger sample of men from which to choose a suitable partner.

LFT isn't something you will overcome overnight. Continue to challenge and dispute your irrational beliefs until you clearly see that they simply don't hold water. Similarly, go over the rational alternatives, debate with yourself until you become convinced that they can stand up to critical examination. Then see for yourself that they produce good results when you push yourself to do things you are not naturally inclined to do, but which you know had better be done, and done *now*! LFT generates procrastination, and procrastination is one of your worst enemies. Don't let it sabotage your efforts to lead the kind of life you want to lead.

In short, there's no magical way to get what you want, nor is there any easy way to change yourself. Work and practise and your determination to keep working at and practising rational thinking and acting against your self-defeating habits will give you a better chance of fulfilling your potential for growth and happiness.

The essence of emotional disturbance

As you go through this book you will come to realize that most human disturbance is a form of demandingness. The emotionally disturbed individual doesn't just want or prefer to win an attractive partner and to become intimately involved with that person. He or she demands, insists, that an encounter with an unusually attractive person of the opposite sex must come about, and fairly soon, that he or she will 'gel' with that person right from the start, and that the chosen person will love him or her devotedly and unstintingly till 'death them do part'. And these demands are just for starters! If you ever meet such an individual, by all means enjoy a date with him or her if that is your inclination; but don't get too emotionally involved if you value your peace of mind! Some neurotic individuals can be great fun to be with. They can be charming, exciting companions when they're in the mood and can be unusually good in bed; we've met one or two ourselves. But unless you are one of those rare individuals who can live happily with a neurotic, take our advice and try anything except becoming too intimately involved with them, especially over the longer term.

The essence of healthy love

We need hardly point out, in this day and age, that there is no such thing as an ideal man – or woman! Nobody is perfect. Love is, in many ways, one of the great forces for good in human life. It can bring immense benefits to the individual as well as to society when it is expressed sanely and healthily. However, when people turn love into a presumed absolute necessity, love becomes demeaned and endangered and the joy of life is diminished. For the outcome of demandingness in love is the creation of anxiety, depression, anger and other unhelpful emotions.

The essence of healthy love is to love fully and committedly in a non-compulsive and non-obligatory manner. So long as your aims and values about loving and being loved are located in the context of *wishes*, that is fine and healthy. But as soon as your wishes and desires for love stray into the irrational domain of absolute mandates or needs, the outcome will almost certainly be some form of happiness-sabotaging emotional conflict which may well drive love away completely.

You can help yourself to find and to stay in a long-term loving relationship with a partner if you convince yourself of the following:

(1) I don't need what I want. A good love relationship may be highly desirable but it isn't an absolute necessity.

(2) Whatever exists, exists. If I fail consistently to relate well to people who mean a lot to me, that is very displeasing. But if that is what always happens, it happens and it's too bad, but it is silly of me to say that it *shouldn't* occur.

(3) I can accept myself as a fallible human being and refuse to rate my personhood as good or bad according to whether my behaviour is good or bad.

(4) When I fail to win what I want, in a love relationship or anything else, I am not a total failure, but only someone who has failed on this occasion. Also, I can learn from my errors to improve my performance and perhaps to win what I want the next time around.

(5) Rational beliefs are factual, realistic, logical and confirmable by experience. Irrational beliefs tend to be unprovable notions with no basis in reality. By learning to practise rational ways of thinking and avoid illogical, irrational ways of thinking, I can reverse my self-upsetting philosophies, accept reality, maximize my freedom of

choice and help myself to lead a happier and more satisfying existence.

What qualities to look for in a man

Let's assume now that you are confidently directing your own existence and are not seriously troubled by anxiety over meeting and dating men, or depressed or angry when the men you do eventually become friendly with turn out to be flawed in ways you consider too serious to be overlooked. And let's assume, also, that LFT is not too serious a problem. Being human, you can hardly expect to banish it completely from your life, but at least you feel that you have it under control. What qualities might you look for in a man that would contribute significantly to establishing a mutually happy, intimate relationship of the kind you are looking for?

We are not about to suggest that you look for a man with a specific set of qualities or characteristics. Obviously, that is a matter for you to decide. Only you know the kind of companion you think would be right for you. As we stressed at the beginning of this chapter, a good man means 'good for me'. What we will try to do is to put forward for your consideration certain aspects of a close relationship which our experience suggests are important in virtually any intimate partnership.

Emotional stability

This is, in our view, one of the most important qualities a man or woman can possess. A person who fluctuates between extremes of mood is not easy to live with, and we doubt whether such a person is happy in his or her own right. Moody people tend to be self-centred, interested in what you and others think of them rather than genuinely interested in you. Demanding frequently to be the centre of attention, they rarely do anything to justify such a degree of interest on the part of others. To be reasonably self-interested is sane and healthy. To be self-centred is to adapt a selfish, I-am-the-only-one-who-counts attitude. Unstable men may, as we noted above, be fun to be with *for a time*, but if you're thinking of making a long-term commitment to one of these emotionally unstable characters, think again!

Communicativeness

This may seem a fairly obvious candidate in any list of desirable characteristics in a partner. The trouble is that the man who is the life and soul of the party may be a very different individual when he is at home with you. He may be able to talk at length about any subject under the sun when he is with you at his club or with a group of friends, but get him home and he can disappear for hours behind a newspaper or become so absorbed in studying the latest additions to his stamp collection that you are lucky if you get a word out of him. Until, that is, he suddenly interrupts what you are doing and demands to know what you've got ready for his supper! Of course, it would be unreasonable to expect a man, once you settle down together, to be a permanent source of scintillating conversation. But there are limits. Silence may be golden, but a steady diet of it night after night can make life leaden. So before making any long-term commitments, make sure that your prospective partner expresses himself when he is with you and is not too tight-lipped. And if he is reticent about expressing his feelings, especially his feelings towards you, find out why. Stiff upper lips were in vogue at one time among the male sex, but not now, thank goodness! The man who never puts his arms around you, kisses you and whispers an endearment or two is just as unacceptable for most women to live with as the man who never leaves you alone. Somewhere in between is the happy medium and it would be a good idea to find it before you get involved with a potential partner. Other qualities such as ambition, drive, sexual prowess, artistic talent, and so on, are highly individual preferences. Some women may rate some of these qualities highly, while others may give them a fairly low priority rating. It is entirely up to you how important such personal qualities and traits or characteristics really are.

Compatibility

Let's face it, practically any two people can live together if they can agree about certain things, or, where they cannot agree, if they can at least work out a mutually acceptable negotiating procedure. Basic compatibility between you means that you already agree upon certain things which you both deem important, whatever these may be. No two people are alike and you would be unwise to look for that perfect partner because the chances are heavily against you ever finding such an animal. As we said above, there is no such thing as an ideal man. However, there is no reason why you should get involved with a man with whom you have to keep constantly trying, constantly negotiating compromises with, when you could find someone with whom you get on just great without having to try so hard! Perfectly compatible you may never be with any mortal, but with a bit of care you can select someone whose main interest and values are very, if not totally, compatible with your own. How much? Well, maybe 70–90 per cent compatible. That degree of overlap between your fundamental values and interests should give you a head start. You probably will still have to negotiate compromises with your partner from time to time, but if you get the 'mix' right to begin with and both you and he are sane, relatively rational and well-adjusted individuals doing what you really want to do, you can look forward to enjoying your lives together to the fullest. That's what you want, isn't it?

How to go about meeting suitable men

Let's assume that you have a pretty good idea of the type of man you would like to find with a view to establishing a good, mutually loving long-term relationship. In this section we will offer you some advice on how to go about the important business of meeting the kind of men you're interested in. Then, we shall conclude with some pertinent, but uncommon comments on where to find potentially suitable men for that relationship you've set your heart on creating.

Men constitute about half the world population. If a woman says she can't meet men, we are pretty sure that she probably has some difficulty in initiating contacts with men or of maintaining contact once she has got over the initial hurdle of meeting one. It's difficult to avoid men; they're everywhere. So why do some women say they never meet any?

Society's sex-role stereotypes

Although things are changing now, the chances are that if you are over 30 you were brought up by parents with fairly rigid ideas derived from the traditional attitudes and sex-role biases prevalent in their day. Your parents in turn got their ideas of right and wrong, what boys were expected to do, how girls were expected to behave, from their parents, and so on. Books, films and the media generally reinforced the traditional (and often foolish) ideas to which many of you were exposed. Already books and articles galore have been written on the subject. Our intention is not to add to what has already been said but to focus your attention on one or two specific aspects of the matter. Even if your upbringing was generally good, you could still have imbibed some misconceptions which are currently inhibiting you from doing the best for yourself.

One such misconception that we frequently encounter is: 'Nice girls wait to be asked'. You've probably heard that one and maybe you still believe it deep down, although you may be reluctant to admit it. It's 'unfeminine' – whatever that means – or, as in older days, 'unladylike'. The women's movement has done a lot to expose the harmful effects of sexist parenting and the over-solicitous ways in which girls were 'protected' from encounters with boys – and all for their own good, of course!

Take control

You don't have to wait to be asked. If you do hang about waiting to be asked, two things could happen, both undesirable: you could easily miss meeting some attractive-looking prospects; and you could be approached by somebody you do *not* consider attractive. On the other hand, by taking the initiative yourself, you do the selecting and you control the timing. If finding a suitable mate for a long-term relationship is important to you, and we are assuming it is, why are you reticent about doing all you can to achieve your goal and with the minimum waste of time? We'll tell you why you are reticent and how you can overcome your tendency to hold back.

Why you hold yourself back

If you have been holding back up till now about taking the initiative in meeting men, and you have still not met the kind of man you are looking for (or hoping will look for you!), you may assume that your negative strategy isn't working and that it is time to reconsider your tactics. If you are selective about the kind of man you want to meet, you are going to have to work that much harder to find him. If you were looking for a good, well-paid job you would actively take steps to find one. You would do some research to find out where these better jobs might be found. You would assess the job markets. You would go for job interviews. You wouldn't just sit around and let the competition step in and get into these good jobs ahead of you.

You had better make the same effort if you are serious about meeting a suitable partner and achieving a good loving long-term relationship with him. The clock isn't going to stop ticking while you just sit back and hope! What is really holding you back from initiating contacts with suitable-looking men is anxiety. You're telling yourself. 'Nice women don't go up to strange men and try to make a date. What would they think of me if I did?' You would feel even more inhibited about approaching some really attractive-looking prospect because of what *he* would think of you! He might even think you were on the 'game' and back away from you, and 'wouldn't that be terrible to think you'd lost a good chance because you were too forward?'

Overcoming your anxiety

Having come this far with us, we feel confident you will see the irrational ideas implied in the self-talk set out in the previous paragraph. If you would like a little help, ask yourself, 'What have I got to lose?' Suppose you met a really good, promising prospect and you made a direct approach to him. Is it really beyond your conversational style to make it clear within minutes at the most that you are not a whore or a pushover but an interesting, intelligent person with whom he could spend an enjoyable half hour? If he is the kind of guy you think he is, he'll be delighted you made the first move. He may even have thought of it himself but was too shy to ask you! If your previous I'll-leave-it-to-him tactics have failed to get you anywhere, what have you got to lose? If your friends think badly of you, let them. Their thoughts can't hurt you. And if some of the men you approach take a dim view of your forwardness, who needs them? You can be glad you have eliminated them from your list of candidates with the minimum waste of your time.

Use the techniques outlined in this book to help you tackle any other emotional block you may find is hampering your efforts to find a suitable man. You are unlikely to find one at the first attempt. Don't give up! Remember, Rome wasn't built in a day. The more you keep honestly trying, the more you will improve your chances of finding the man who is right for you.

The spontaneous pick-up

You probably have your own ideas about where to meet men. Dances, parties, social outings of various kinds are all good ways of making contact with the opposite sex. Blind dates, dating agency selections (which are virtually the same thing) are rather hit-and-miss methods. But what's the most efficient way of meeting the largest feasible representative sample of men, so that you can make the best possible choice? Our answer may surprise you: it's the spontaneous pick-up!

If you live or work in or around a large city, begin by looking for men wherever you happen to be at the time. It may be a restaurant, department store, library, bus terminal or railway station. Many of the men you encounter in these places you will be able to eliminate at first sight. They will be obviously unsuitable for a variety of reasons. Others you see may look somewhat promising, but the man you are after is not likely to be of the run-of-the-mill type. You will, eventually, spot a few interesting-looking possibilities. When you do see someone interesting, attractive, intelligent-looking, go up and speak to him. Don't do that if he is already accompanied by another woman, of course! Why do we recommend taking the initiative yourself? Well, first, it's the quickest method we know. You're already there, you are suitably dressed, you don't have to start preparing to go out. The scene is already set for you. All you have to do is to come on and say your piece!

Second, if you actively pick up strange men you are being far more selective than if you sit passively around waiting for one of them to pick you up! When you do the picking up, you are in charge. You pick and choose whom *you* wish to meet, whereas with the other way you are the

40

object of someone else's wishes – and you've no means of knowing in advance what they are! Which do you think is the safer way to meet the kind of man you are after?

Third, the spontaneous pick-up gives you the widest possible sample of men to choose from. In the street, almost anywhere in public, you have thousands of men to select from. It follows that if you persist with your attempts, you are far more likely to meet a man of the calibre you are looking for than if you opt for the passive techniques of waiting patiently for a man to pick you up. And, as we mentioned before, if you allow yourself to be picked up, you will often be picked up by the kind of man you definitely don't want to get involved with. All things considered, the spontaneous pick-up is your best bet, and your safest bet, for meeting at least a few promising prospects in the minimum amount of time and with the least amount of preparatory effort. Use it in conjunction with your more conventional techniques if you wish, and you should find on the law of averages at least a few good prospects. Remember, though, not to take any unnecessary risks. Safety first is our watchword.

After the pick-up, what then?

You are presumably bright and sophisticated enough to know how to engage in conversation a man with whom you've discovered some common ground. However, before you get to get round to exchanging confidences, don't rush things! Before you go out with him, ascertain a few pertinent details about your prospect. Get his home phone number and his home address. Check them out. Make sure he has an address! Half an hour spent chatting in a coffee bar should give you a good idea of whether you want to get to know him better. If you decide it probably isn't worth your while you can plead another engagement and leave.

We hope we have given you food for thought in this chapter. It may be hard, at least for a little while after you first start working at it, to change some of your previous ways. However, in the long run it will be harder on you if you don't change the inhibiting habits which have prevented you from achieving what you want from life. Accept the challenge to take control of your life. It won't kill you if you don't, but on the other hand your life could really improve if you determinedly go after what you really want, using the advice set before you in this book. What have you got to lose?

Summary

(1)   A 'good man' is a man who is good for *you*, and not necessarily what other people might consider 'good'.

(2)   There are two major kinds of obstacle to finding a 'good man'. The first kind consists of various obstacles created by, or inherited by, the society and culture you live in. Because these obstacles are socially maintained, they can be changed through social or political action, but they are generally very resistant to change.

(3)   The other main group of obstacles is the one we are chiefly concerned with. This group consists of various disturbed emotions which are created and maintained by several basic irrational ideas which people believe about themselves, others and the world they live in. Unlike the first group of obstacles, this second group of disturbed emotions can be replaced, after much hard practice, by more rational ideas and healthier feelings which aid and abet happier living for oneself and one's associates. In the context of finding a good partner for a long-term intimate relationship, the main saboteurs of that enterprise are anxiety and low frustration tolerance (LFT), or, as it is sometimes called, discomfort anxiety. Both these obstacles to beginning and sustaining a good relationship can be overcome by the methods outlined in this chapter.

(4)   Three main qualities stand out as of paramount importance when seriously looking for a suitable partner for a mutually satisfactory long-term intimate relationship. These three important qualities are: emotional stability; communicativeness; and compatibility.

(5)   The influence of sex-role stereotypes on your upbringing may exercise an inhibiting effect on your taking an active role in finding a suitable man with whom to have a long-term relationship. By focusing on rational ways of thinking you can overcome your anxiety about what other people might think about you and thus take control of the situation.

(6)   Having encouraged you to take the initiative in meeting men, we then put forward our suggestions on where to meet men. We introduced the idea of the spontaneous pick-up and showed you how, if properly handled, this method was by far the most efficient way available to meet men of the calibre you want.

(7)   Finally, having successfully made contact with a promising prospect, we offered advice on how to behave during the initial encounter, emphasizing certain steps you should take to safeguard yourself from being tricked into a dangerous or unwanted relationship.

3

'I Can't Face the Risk of Rejection'

When a woman – or a man for that matter – says 'I can't face the risk of rejection!', meaning rejection in love, we can usually draw two valid conclusions. First, the person concerned has enjoyed a good love relationship with a chosen partner, has experienced reciprocation for a time and then is rejected. How do we know this will turn out to be true? Well, in our experience, a person who enters a love relationship for the first time is not usually concerned about the possibility of rejection. If the feelings of love are reciprocated, both the partners feel pretty good about their relationship, and the possibility of rejection rarely occurs to them. Many people recall their first time in love as one of the happiest times of their lives. So it isn't the first-timers who are afraid to face the risk of rejection.

The second deduction we make when someone tells us that she can't face the risk of rejection, is that the person concerned really would like to get involved once more in a love relationship but is so afraid of the consequences of another rejection that she is just not prepared to take the chance. Most of us are biologically programmed to feel attracted to members of the opposite sex and to form and maintain over a period of time intimate ties with those for whom we feel a strong affinity. That being so, it doesn't appear to be so much a question of some newly acquired inability to 'let themselves go' and fall in love a second or third time which bothers some women, but rather a very strong reluctance to let themselves do so, especially if a previous love affair has turned out badly for them. 'I might pick the wrong man again!' is the theme song of these women and the unspoken inference behind it is: 'And I would be rejected again. And that would mean I would be hurt again. And because it was so horrible the first time, I daren't risk it happening to me again!' Now, we think it sad that some women who really want to love and to be loved have decided to turn their backs on the possibility of enjoying one of the most exciting and enriching experiences a human being can have. It is also unnecessary to cut yourself off from taking a chance on love for the very good reason that, even if you were to be rejected, neither the rejection itself nor the reasons for it could possibly cause you to feel so emotionally upset that you vow 'never again'. We are not denying that you will feel very sad following the break-up of a relationship you wanted to continue. You will feel pain, real pain, as almost anyone who has experienced it will readily agree. But it isn't the rejection, and it isn't the reasons for the rejection, however unpalatable these may be to you personally, that cause your emotional turmoil when the man you loved tells you it's all over. That is painful enough, as we know. No, there is something else that happens, something that goes on inside your head about what happened to you, and it is this 'something else' that adds to the pain you already feel after being rejected. It is this 'something else' that is the real culprit behind your decision not to risk entering another relationship.

Since it isn't the reasons your partner gave you for ending the relationship that cause you to feel so worthless and anxious we don't propose to spend time discussing them. You can be rejected for practically any reason, and sometimes you won't even be given a reason! There are several good books already available which detail some of the more common reasons for the break-up of love relationships and outline the steps women can take to make their love relationships more satisfying as well as to avoid getting involved with the wrong men in the first place. Quite readable and interesting are the two books by Drs Connell Cowan and Melvyn Kinder entitled *Smart Women, Foolish Choices*, (1985), and *Women Men Love, Women Men Leave*, (1987), both published by Bantam Books. Also worth mentioning is Robin Norwood's *Women Who Love Too Much*, (publ. Arrow Books, 1985) although we don't agree with everything she says. But we cannot help but wonder how many women can actually use these books. If you have just emerged from a relationship which has come unstuck you are unlikely to be in any great hurry to get involved in another one. There will still be too many tender spots inside you, and until you successfully tackle the emotional problems surrounding your rejection, you are unlikely to make much headway with improving a future relationship. For that reason we think this book of ours goes beyond the others mentioned; we show you how to get over your emotional problems first, by teaching you how to recognize and uproot the irrational ideas which sooner or later will get in the way of starting and maintaining the kind of loving, intimate relationship you presumably want. And more important still, we hope to help you acquire a philosophy of life which, if you consistently practise it, will enable you to avoid seriously upsetting yourself about virtually anything that might happen to you for the rest of your life.

Now let's get down to the fundamentals of rejection. Only one person runs your life: *you*! If you are afraid to take a chance on love because you were rejected once and you felt very hurt, or if you are afraid of being taken over by a man, of 'losing yourself', we will show you why such fears are groundless. If you really want to make a commitment to a man and still retain a commitment to yourself as an individual, to those things you truly value and to your most cherished aspirations, you can learn to do just that by carefully studying and practising the RET guidelines set out for you here.

Getting to grips with rejection

It is understandable that if you have felt hurt, have experienced real pain as a result of being rejected by a partner with whom you enjoyed a good relationship, you will feel reluctant, to put it mildly, to throw yourself into another relationship. Even if you still want and hope for some future love relationship in your life, you may well be asking yourself how you can be sure it won't end like the last one did. You'll never again want to feel again that despair, that misery, when the man you loved turned his back on you.

You don't need guarantees!

Unfortunately, there are no guarantees of happiness in love, or indeed anywhere else. All life carries an element of risk, and, like it or not, we would be wise to recognize and accept this. No, you can't be sure that if you take a chance with some new future partner you won't experience rejection a second time. You may, or you may not. But we are going to try to show you that you don't *have* to be sure of succeeding in love, or anything else you try for, and that, win or lose, you need never be utterly miserable or despairing about anything for the rest of your life. If you can persuade yourself that the fundamental ideas of RET can be upheld and if you can really believe in the philosophy we teach you in this book, you will no longer be afraid to take a chance on love, regardless of whether it is the second, the third or the thirtieth time. Once you fully accept yourself unconditionally and once you realize that life is for living, you will feel free to throw yourself into even the most intense kind of romantic love relationship without having to feel certain in advance that it is the real thing and that it will endure forever. The more you show willingness to take risks (but with your eyes fully open, of course!) in entering relationships, the more you will improve your chances of success. For your partner will perceive your lack of vulnerability to rejection and he, in turn, will be encouraged to feel more free in expressing his own feelings. Each of you will become more 'visible' to the other, with mutually beneficial results for your relationship. But first, we turn our attention to the 'nuts and bolts' of rejection and show you what you can do about it should it ever happen to you. Many people, perhaps most, ourselves included, have experienced rejection and the pain that goes with it, so we know what we are talking about.

What we mean by 'rejection'

Let's make one thing clear; when we talk about rejection, we do not mean the final parting of the ways following a long period of gradual disintegration in the relationship. What we mean by rejection is what most other people who have experienced it mean; the *sudden* end to what had seemed a very happy relationship! When the end comes, it comes with shattering suddenness! And you just can't believe it. But then the reality hits you and that is the moment when the pain really begins. But it is more than just the pain of sadness you might feel following a bereavement, for example. You would normally and naturally go through a period of grief, sometimes intense grief and mourning, if you lost a very good relationship with some beloved partner. When we talk about the pain of rejection we are indicating a degree of misery and despair so intense that in severe cases it requires several days in hospital under sedation. We hope it won't come to that should you ever suffer rejection. So, to help you to avoid becoming emotionally devastated if you ever do suffer a sudden rejection from someone you previously were very happy with, we will take you through a fairly typical rejection scenario step by step. We will show you how to identify the mental processes which lead to severe emotional disturbances such as anxiety, self-hatred and depression, and what you can do to prevent the natural feelings of sadness and loss, which you will normally experience following rejection, from escalating into overwhelming emotional misery.

Some typical feelings following rejection

As we noted above, it is common and natural to feel sad when we have been rejected by someone we love. Some writers have likened the feelings following rejection to the feelings of grief occasioned by bereavement. If sadness and regret were all that people felt after rejection, there would be no problem. However, it is not uncommon for people who have suffered rejection to report that the period following the rejection was the most miserable time in their entire life. Why is this so? In a moment we shall explain how sadness and regret are escalated into despair and misery. But first, to get a better idea of just how intense a person's emotional turmoil can become following a rejection in love, listen to what some women have reported feeling after a break-up they neither wanted nor expected.

'I was so miserable after the break-up with Glen that I spent sleepness nights longing for him to come back. He never did and after ten weeks I'd lost so much weight that my doctor suspected cancer.'

'I used to cry myself to sleep every night for nearly ten months after

Tom left me for that girl. It was so good when we were together; how could he do that to me after we were so close?'

'Ted was everything I ever wanted in a man. I know he had his faults like everyone else, I suppose, but I still think – in fact I *know* – that Ted is the only man for me. To go with any other man would be such a comedown compared to those deliriously happy times we spent together that it would seem like a betrayal of everything I valued and treasured about Ted. For me, it's Ted or nobody.'

Without exception, all these women fantasized about getting back with the men they loved long after it was clear to everyone else that these men were never coming back. The more they fantasized, the more they prolonged their own agony. In case you're wondering, men behave just as foolishly when it is they who are rejected and the pain they experience can be just as debilitating. In some ways, men sometimes behave even more foolishly, as when they go berserk and try to kill their ex-girlfriends and then themselves afterwards. You have now gained some idea of the misery some people go through after the break-up of a love relationship. We have introduced you already to the A-B-C model of emotional disturbance RET therapists use when dealing with clients' emotional problems. So let's see now how we would handle a client who is emotionally disturbed following the break-up of a love relationship.

The A-B-C of rejection

In the material that follows we shall incorporate elements of our own life experiences to help us to clarify for you in a fairly dramatic manner the stages a person may go through following the sudden ending of what had been a very happy love relationship.

Tracy, a 29-year-old public relations officer met Don, a 36-year-old architect at a reception given by the hotel and leisure group which Tracy worked for. Tracy was single, while Don had been married but was now divorced. Strongly attracted to one another, a full-blown love relationship quickly developed between Don and Tracy. Tracy had gone out with several men before she met Don, but had never met anyone who really turned her on like Don did. She was over the moon. They had many interests in common, and liked the same things; they went on beach picnics, they went dancing in fashionable discos, they went on shopping sprees together. Although they got on well enough with each other's friends, they liked nothing better than to be alone together. Tracy had never felt so happy and Don seemed happy, too, always there, attentive and loving.

The break-up came with shattering suddenness. Without omitting essential details, we will now summarize the stages in the breaking-up of a relationship and show how RET can help significantly to overcome the emotional turmoil which so often is a consequence of rejection.

A stands for the activating event

Don and Tracy arranged to meet in a café. Tracy could tell right away from Don's demeanour that something was wrong but she had no inkling of the shock that was soon to come. Sitting in dazed disbelief, Tracy heard Don announce that the relationship was over. He had met someone else, he couldn't say much about it because, as he put it, 'I don't want to hurt you, Tracy, any more than I have to'. Numbed with shock, it was a few minutes before Tracy realized that Don had quietly left the café and had walked out of her life. So, at point A, we have the break-up. One partner suddenly announces the relationship is over and walks out.

C stands for the emotional and behavioural consequences

Hollow-eyed, gaunt and looking the picture of misery, Tracy came for help. The first thing to realize is that if you have an experience like Tracy's, it is entirely *appropriate* to feel intense sorrow, regret, sadness and even annoyance and frustration at being prevented from getting what you very much wanted. Do not underplay the sense of grief, of deep loss. Admit the pain. The pain of loss is real, and one of the most intense you are ever likely to suffer. Let the pain and grief come out. As the pain eases with the passage of time, you will still feel sad, regretful and frustrated. But you will be motivated to do something about it, perhaps to try and get back with the person who rejected you, if that is possible. If it is highly unlikely that you will win back your ex-lover, you will begin to consider other possibilities, such as looking for someone else with whom you could have the kind of relationship you want.

Unfortunately many who experience rejection go far beyond feeling sadness and grief. They become depressed, they feel intense despair and are overcome with inertia. Intense anxiety ('What if the next one ends the same way?') and suicidal thoughts prevent the individual from breaking free from his or her misery and doing something constructive about finding a new partner. We call these reactions to rejection *inappropriate*, first, because such reactions are not caused by the rejection itself at point A, and second, because they are self-defeating: they do nothing to help the individual to get back into leading a normal life or to actively look for an adequate replacement for the lost relationship.

B stands for your belief system

Well, if these reactions of despair, and so on, are not caused by being rejected by someone you dearly loved, what does cause them? As Tracy remarked: 'If the misery I went through wasn't caused by Don leaving me, I can't imagine what did cause it!' And that brings us to the crux of the matter – point B.

B stands for what you believe about the things that happen to you. The way you appraise or evaluate events in your life as good, bad or neutral springs from your core values, beliefs and previous experiences. There are basically two kinds of belief: rational and irrational.

Your rational beliefs tend to be factual, realistic, logical and self-helping or productive. They help you to achieve your goals. Irrational beliefs, by contrast, are non-factual, unreal and unrealistic, illogical and self-defeating or unproductive in the sense of preventing you from achieving your goals in life.

Because thoughts, feelings and behaviour are all interrelated and interacting, *rational* beliefs about life events promote *appropriate* emotional responses and behaviours. *Irrational* beliefs about life events bring about *inappropriate* emotional responses and self-defeating actions and behaviours. It follows that an individual who becomes emotionally disturbed about some event or happening in his or her life, such as rejection or the break-up of a valued relationship, does so because that individual believes strongly in some set of ideas which simply don't make sense. The way to help that person get over his or her emotional disturbance is to identify and uproot the irrational beliefs and replace them with more rational convictions. These new convictions, when acted upon and practised consistently, will help the person to surrender his or her negative and harmful emotions and to behave in ways which will help the achievement of valued life goals. Let's see how this would work in a case like Tracy's.

Rational and irrational beliefs about rejection

Essentially, an individual who is emotionally disturbed about rejection brings two sets of beliefs to the activating event or precipitating situation at A: First, a rational, appropriate set: 'I don't like the break-up of this relationship. It was great while it lasted. I really wish it had never happened to me and I feel very, very displeased. How annoying and frustrating it is and how very sad that it should end like this.' Beliefs like these are not disputable; they are confirmable by an appeal to the facts. You have lost something extremely valuable and important to you and your response is appropriately sad, regretful and frustrating.

The real turmoil begins when the rejected person believes a set of highly *irrational* beliefs like the following:

(1)   This break-up *must* not happen to me!
(2)   It's horrible that the break-up has happened.
(3)   I can't stand it breaking up like this when it could have been such a glorious relationship.
(4)   Since the relationship did break up there must be something rotten about me because otherwise I would have succeeded in getting my boyfriend to love me as I wanted him to.
(5)   I'll *never* be able to make it with a good man again.

The contributing factor is obviously the relationship break-up. Without it there would be nothing for these irrational beliefs to latch on to. But given the two together – the intense feelings of loss augmented by these highly irrational convictions – the result can hardly be anything other than emotional mayhem!

As you will have gathered, we have now revealed the identity of the culprit we previously hinted would turn out to be the real cause of your emotional misery as well as the inspiration of your decision never to risk an involvement with some new person in future. These five irrational ideas constitute the root cause of that emotional devastation which afflicts many people following rejection in love. The obvious question you will now be asking is: 'Well, what do we do about this culprit, this cause of our anxiety, despair and self-downing?'

Our answer is, go to D! We've taught you the A-B-C of emotional disturbance. Now comes D, which stands for disputing the validity of those irrational beliefs by asking if they make sense. Can they be proved? Are they logical, factual, realistic? Are these beliefs likely to help you achieve your goals in life, or are they likely to prove self-defeating? Can they be rationally upheld? If not, then we drop them and replace them with beliefs for which there is verifiable evidence.

Are irrational beliefs not just mistaken beliefs? By no means! They are mistaken, of course, but irrational beliefs go far beyond being merely mistaken. Irrational beliefs are beliefs which simply don't make sense. They are highly exaggerated, illogical and unrealistic. They invariably carry some aspect of *demandingness* in them, like demanding that the world must be different to what it actually is, or demanding that some unpleasant event *must* not happen. In Chapter 1 we introduced you to the three main irrational ideas which in one form or another are the core of virtually all emotional disturbance. The five irrational ideas which we identified above as the real cause of the anxiety, despair and self-downing following rejection in love, all contain one or more of the three main irrational ideas. See if you can spot them!

Apart from their fundamental difference in content, ideas which are merely mistaken, as against ideas which are completely irrational, do not normally cause you emotional distress. For example, if you arrived by car on the continent of Europe intending to drive to Paris, and you drove east into Germany and then Poland because you were under the impression that Paris lay somewhere east of Warsaw, you would eventually realize your mistake and turn round. You would probably feel annoyed at the time and effort you had wasted, but you could hardly regard this as a great tragedy.

Irrational – nor merely mistaken – ideas about yourself, other people and the world cause you emotional distress and impel you to act in various unproductive and self-defeating ways. It follows that if you wish to change the way you feel, to get rid of unhelpful, painful negative feelings such as anxiety, depression, guilt or self-denigration, and to eliminate unhelpful behaviour patterns such as inertia, procrastination, over-indulgence and lack of self-discipline then you had better begin by challenging and disputing the irrational ideas which fuel those disturbed emotions and behaviours. And that's where point D comes in.

Rejection: disputing irrational beliefs

At point D you ask yourself for evidence or proof in support of your irrational ideas; if you really think about it you'll see that you won't be able to find any. Let's show you what we mean by disputing the irrational beliefs we mentioned on page 50.

(1) 'This break-up must not happen to me.'

Where is the evidence that a relationship *must* not break up? If there was such a law, no relationship would ever break up. If break-ups exist, they exist. Too bad! Reality is reality. It's preferable if this break-up doesn't happen, but there is no reason why it must not occur.

(2) 'It's horrible that the break-up has happened.'

Prove that it's horrible when a relationship breaks up! Prove that it's awful (not undesirable or very sad and unfortunate, which we agree that it is), but really terrible, 100 per cent bad? Think what other unfortunate things could happen to you: like dying of cancer; being severely crippled for life in a road accident; being thrown into gaol in some foreign country, or taken hostage. Words like 'awful' and 'horrible' mean not only more than totally bad, but also that whatever is designated horrible or awful or terrible *must* not exist. We've already made the point; what exists, exists. It is therefore illogical to demand that because something unpleasant happens, it must not exist. It's unfortunate that the break-up has happened, but hardly horrible.

(3) 'I can't stand it breaking up when it could have been such a glorious relationship.'

When someone declares 'I can't stand such-and-such' they are predicting an imminent demise. Does that happen? Do they come apart at the seams, or do they evaporate before your very eyes? No such fate has befallen anyone we know, including those who have actually suffered rejection and the break-up of a valued love relationship. The only logical, supportable answer you can give is: 'Yes, I can stand it. I'll never like being rejected but it's not demeaning unless I foolishly tell myself it is, and I can still find happiness, perhaps a great deal of happiness, with somebody else. And if I don't I can still find some happiness, even by myself.'

(4) 'Since the relationship did break up there must be something rotten about me because otherwise I would have succeeded in getting my boyfriend to love me as I wanted him to.'

How does it follow that I am a rotten person because of my ex-partner? Even if I contributed to disrupting our relationship, or my ex-partner became tired or bored with me, how does that make me a no-good person? If indeed I failed in this particular relationship, I can probably learn something from my failure, but I, my totality as a human being, cannot be judged or rated on the basis of a few traits or abilities. My acts can be evaluated as good or bad by other people according to their particular goals or purposes, but I am me, a complex human being with millions of changing characteristics who cannot be given any kind of global rating. My self-acceptance is not at stake here. Consequently, I cannot be denigrated or put down by the actions of another person or feel 'wounded' or 'demeaned' by their rejection of me, or by failure to live up to my own, or their expectations. Since most downing often involves self-downing, if I feel like a worm because I have been rejected by someone whose love I very much wanted to keep, that is because I foolishly make my self-worth dependent upon retaining that person's love. No relationship can ever be worth the sacrifice of my self-acceptance.

(5) 'I'll never be able to make it with a good man again.'

'Never' is a pretty strong word! Of course, I may never make it with that particular person who rejected me, but how does that prove I can never make it with someone else? I'm no angel, but then neither is anybody else, and even if my ex-partner gave up on me because I had some trait or quality he found unacceptable, there may be hundreds of other potential partners who will find my qualities quite acceptable. Everybody is different, we're individuals, and there is no evidence that I can be happy with only a particular person or with only *that* person with whom I'd previously been happy. One thing is sure, though. If I sit on my rump all day and moan about the injustice of it all and convince myself that, because I'm rejected, I am totally undeserving of any happiness again, I probably won't win myself another partner and get a good relationship going with that person. So, let me forget that 'never' and get myself out into the mainstream of life again and see what happens!

A new cognitive effect

Provided you persist at challenging and disputing the irrational ideas which made and keep you depressed, anxious and self-hating after you've experienced a sudden and unwanted rejection, you will acquire a new outlook, what we term in RET a new 'cognitive effect' (at point E). That simply means you have given up some of your more irrational ideas and are now experiencing more appropriate feelings and acting in more self-helping ways. The more you work at and practise, in both thought and action, disputing your irrational ideas, the stronger will your new more rational philosophy become. Just as regular physical exercise builds up your body muscles, so will regular exercise with RET techniques help you to acquire emotional muscle. Then, should you ever be unfortunate enough to be rejected by someone you loved, you will know how to cope with it.

'I must find the explanation.'

It is by no means uncommon for individuals suffering the pain of rejection to spend endless hours raking over the ashes to find the explanation for what happened. Such an enterprise will almost always prove unsuccessful and act more as a brake on recovery than actually promote it. It is almost as if finding the right explanation will magically make everything 'all right' again and offering it to one's ex-partner will compel the partner to take one back again.

There are several good reasons why compulsively seeking for the perfect explanation will do you more harm than good. First, the longer you mull over what went wrong, the longer you will prolong the pain associated with the loss of the relationship.

Second, you are unlikely to find the 'correct' explanation because your own biased perceptions will not necessarily pick up the salient clues. You may tend, for the same reason, to focus your attention on aspects of the relationship which were unimportant or really had nothing to do with the real reasons which compelled your partner to break off the relationship.

Third, women tend to blame themselves more than their partners for the failure of their relationships. Even before it gets that far, if a prospective date promises to meet up with a woman friend and then fails to turn up at the appointed time the woman will often wonder what is wrong with *her*, what did she say or do to put him off? It seldom seems to occur to these women that the prospective date might have got 'cold feet' or changed his mind for reasons entirely unconnected with them. If your relationship with someone breaks up, it may be for reasons which have more to do with your ex-partner's inadequacies than with any failings of yours.

Fourth, even if, by some remote chance, you do come up with the perfect explanation of what went wrong and you dash over to tell ex-lover how you now have it all figured out, he is hardly likely to fall at your feet and beg you to take him back. He is more likely to say: 'Yes, that's exactly right. You've got it. That is why I left you, and why I'm not coming back – ever!'

Fifth, and the most important of all the reasons why you are largely wasting your time and prolonging your misery, is that by obsessively searching for the perfect explanation for the break-up you divert yourself from what should be your main, overriding purpose: not to figure out what went wrong and why, but to identify and uproot the irrational ideas with which you've been plaguing yourself over the years and which are the real source and mainstay of your current misery. Once you have accomplished *that* task, you probably won't care too much about untangling the complex web of motives and circumstances which constituted the reason for the break-up of your relationship. It simply won't matter that much any more. You can still calmly review your part in the relationship and maybe learn a few hints on what might be helpful the next time round and what might not. Convert the situation into a learning experience. But as for finding that perfect explanation – forget it!

Reframe your rejection

We would like to offer you another means of helping you to climb out of your depression and despondency about ever being happy with anyone again involving thinking differently about (or *reframing*) rejection. Continue to dispute your irrational beliefs, the whole object of which is to rid yourself of those disturbed emotions and behaviours as quickly as possible and get back to the business of living, of enjoying and running your life the way you want to run it. That is your goal. In addition, we suggest that you carefully think through and carry out the following suggestions:

First, when one is rejected and the loss of love leads to acute self-downing, the rejected partner views himself or herself as totally worthless. Typically, one is saying to oneself: 'There must be something terribly wrong with me, otherwise why should I have been abandoned like this and the love I enjoyed taken away from me!' The essence of self-downing is the conviction that one is rejected as a person, as a human being, and that one is undeserving of being loved in future, especially by the person who did the rejecting. If you think about it, you will see that it is highly unlikely that your ex-partner is rejecting you totally as a person. He may be, but the chances are that he only wants you to stay away from him. Regardless of his reasons for breaking with you (and remember, his reasons might have nothing to do with you, personally), the message you are receiving loud and clear is: 'I don't want you around any more. Just stay away from me!'

You haven't become worthless in *his* eyes, you haven't suddenly become a person without any good points whatever! If you feel worthless, it is because *you* think so. 'I'm no good, I'm no good!' you keep repeating to yourself, and so long as you keep that up, you are bound to see yourself as a tragic figure. How can the fact that your beloved has turned away from you possibly make you a wretch? You are you, a human being with millions of traits and characteristics. You cannot be given worth by an external agent. Nor, by the same token, can your value or worth to yourself be taken away from you. You can accept yourself unconditionally as a human being with intrinsic value; that is, you have value to yourself and the right to live. You don't need other people's approval or permission to live and be happy. You cannot be validated as a person by anyone other than yourself. Once you grasp that and make it a part of what you truly believe, you will realize that rejection is really *self-rejection*. You put yourself down. Nobody can put you down; you do it to yourself. In other words, being rejected doesn't make you a rejectee. This is what we mean by reframing rejection. You begin to look upon your experience as a challenge instead of a horror. You begin to look for the benefits you can gain from it instead of dwelling only on its disadvantages.

Second, don't make the relationship you had, or the next relationship you have, the be-all and end-all of your life. Of course, they are important, but there are other kinds of relationships which you might wish to maintain, such as your relationships with your friends, your occupation or work colleagues and your social contacts. These other relationships can be of value to you and help you recover from the pain following the loss of love. Becoming creatively absorbed in your work, sport, hobbies, and so on, can do wonders to distract you from dwelling too much on your lost love.

Third, avoid spending much of your time looking back on your happiest memories of your time with your ex-partner. We believe you when you tell us that these carefree, sunny days you spent together were some of the happiest days of your entire life, that you felt more alive than at any time since. But put those memories of halcyon days past into cold storage for the time being. They won't fade or disappear! The more you focus on what a great time you had then, the worse you will tend to feel as you look at your life now. By dwelling obsessively on those happier days you will be reviving your feelings of self-pity at a time when you are beginning to make good headway against them. So stop daydreaming about what was, and what might have been. When you are back on the upbeat once more, and not before, you can permit yourself an occasional glimpse back. And if you are involved with somebody new by then, you may well find that those past memories no longer seem like the magical kingdom you once thought they were.

Fourth, another part of the process of reframing rejection is to focus on the disadvantages or less attractive aspects of the person whose love you have lost. You may have thought he was God's gift to women while you and he were together, but we have yet to meet a perfect man, and your ex-lover is unlikely to be the first. Compare his disadvantages with the advantages some other possible partners possess. Seek out new partners! Don't waste your valuable time feeling sorry for yourself!

Finally, if, in spite of your efforts to break free from your feelings of depression, self-downing or anxiety, you still miserably ruminate about your lost love and think only of what you *must* do to get that particular partner back, you can help yourself overcome this dire need for a particular person by reading *How to Break Your Addiction to a Person* by Howard Halpern (Bantam Books, 1983). Packed with good practical advice, this is a book we can strongly recommend if you have been rejected but cannot bring yourself to accept the fact and let go. How do you know if you're addicted to your ex-lover? Well, apart from the continuing pain you experience day in day out, if you stubbornly keep telling yourself 'You're the only one for me. I don't want anybody else but you. It's *your* love I need. Nobody else could ever make me feel the way I do about you', and so on, you can take it you are addicted. We hope that by now you will realize that every single one of these exclamations is either nonsensical or unprovable. Practise, practise the techniques of disputing your self-defeating beliefs that you must have a particular person's love to be happy as well as those other irrational beliefs which keep you feeling low and self-pitying. Go after them and keep working at challenging them until you came to see them for the illusions they are. You know life is for living, right? You know your time on this earth is limited. So why waste even a minute of your precious time or suffer even a minute of needless pain by crying over spilt milk?

Acquiring a rational outlook

As we stated above, the object of disputing, plus those other insights we suggested, is to help you acquire a new, more rational way of viewing yourself and your experiences so that you deal with the various problems that arise in your life in a sensible, productive manner without upsetting yourself emotionally in the process. What we are saying is that if you vigorously and vehemently persist in disputing your irrational beliefs at point D about the unpleasant events at point A which happen to you (such as rejection in love), then you will eventually arrive at point E. You will achieve a cognitive effect – a new, rational way of thinking about what originally happened to you at point A. In effect, the cognitive effect consists of rational answers in a general more philosophical form to the questions you brought to bear on your irrational beliefs when you disputed them at point D. You will now be able to state with conviction your new rational beliefs about your rejection, in terms such as the following:

'Losing the love I had was indeed a painful experience and I wish that it had not happened. It is sad that it happened, but it isn't an unmitigated disaster.'

'My beloved may have had his own reasons for rejecting me, which may, or may not, have had something to do with the way I behaved. But whatever his reasons or prejudices may have been, I am not a worm because he withdrew from me.'

'I was very happy with our relationship while it lasted, but there is no reason why it absolutely had to continue indefinitely, no matter how much I would have preferred it to. My ex-lover found me attractive when we first met, and I have no reason to suppose that I will not appear attractive to other men I may meet in future. It is foolish to imagine I can be happy with only one particular man. There are many men out there in the world with whom I could probably create a long-lasting deeply caring, loving relationship. The sooner I begin to look, the sooner I may find a man for me!'

You will also feel differently. If you persist with these rational ways of thinking, you will achieve a new emotional and behavioural effect. What this means is that you will no longer wallow in self-pity over the loss of love, nor will you sit around the house convinced that you'll never find another man who could make you feel as happy as you were with your former partner. Instead, you will feel much more motivated to do something constructive about replacing your lost love by going out and looking for someone else, without feeling in any way guilty about doing so.

You might even consider trying to get back with your ex-partner if you think there are grounds for recementing your relationship with him. Let's suppose you still love him. And let's suppose you discover that he won't take you back. It is important to realize that you don't *need* reciprocation of your love when you continue to feel strong feelings of love for your partner after the relationship has ended. You presumably loved your ex-partner for the qualities of mind and character he possessed and all those other uniquely personal traits and values which captured your admiration. He may have changed in some ways, most of us do as we gain more experience of life, but he is most unlikely to have changed out of all recognition. If you truly loved your former partner before you parted, there is no reason why you cannot continue to do so now, calmly and non-desperately, even if there is little or no reciprocation. You don't *need* it! This doesn't mean that you seal yourself off from new contacts, new partners. The idea, once commonly believed, that you could truly love only one person of the opposite sex at any one time, is now widely accepted as the myth it always was. The point is, you can still strongly prefer to get back with your ex-partner, but you don't *need* him, and there is no reason why you can't actively seek other suitable partners and enjoy their company without anxiety, guilt or shame. Probably the sooner you do just that, the better!

Summary

(1)   Rejection in love is a painful experience and you will naturally feel sad over the loss of a love relationship you wished to continue. How we feel is a direct result of how we think, and many people in this situation will convince themselves of such irrational beliefs as 'It's terrible to be rejected', 'It *must* not happen', 'I must be a very unlovable person for this to happen to me' and 'I'll *never* know happiness again with anyone else'. These beliefs lead to self-defeating emotional states such as depression, anxiety and self-hate. (2)   By illustrating how to dispute these irrational beliefs, we showed you how to uproot them and replace them with rational convictions. Thinking rationally about being rejected won't make you like it, but your dislike will motivate you to act constructively to improve your situation, either by trying to get back with your ex-

partner, or, if that is not feasible, to actively, and without guilt, seek new relationships.

(3)   We emphasize that love is desirable but that you don't *need* it, especially not the love of any particular person, and that you can love several different people at one and the same time.

(4)   We introduced the idea of reframing (or thinking differently about) rejection so that you see it more as a challenge than as a horror.

(5)   Acquiring a rational outlook will enable you to take the risk of finding a new partner and help you to accept disappointment in love (should it happen) without unduly upsetting yourself.

4

'I Just Get Jealous and I Don't Know Why'

The word 'jealousy' has two quite distinct, almost opposite, senses, and it is a pity that the same word has to do duty for both of these senses. The word as we use it probably goes a little bit beyond what most people understand by it. So, to avoid possible misunderstanding, we will designate the two meanings of jealousy by the expressions 'rational jealousy' and 'irrational jealousy'. We will show you what we mean by these new terms and why it is important that you clearly see the difference between them.

Irrational jealousy

This is what is generally understood by 'jealousy'. Next to anger, which, as you will see, frequently accompanies jealousy, more relationships are destroyed by jealousy and more lives are made miserable through jealousy than probably any other single factor. Jealousy – and its twin, possessiveness – are often the direct cause of so much needless unhappiness in marriage and other kinds of intimate relationship that we feel justified in devoting a whole chapter to pinpointing the causes of jealousy and indicating what you can do to rid yourself of it, or to help your partner fight against it. Let us first take a look at how jealous people behave.

Self-downing

The most salient characteristic exhibited by jealous people is lack of self-acceptance. They seem to have little or no sense of their value or worth to themselves. A woman once told us: 'I don't count. As long as I have a roof over my head and enough food to stay alive, that's all that matters.' This self-demeaning attitude follows logically from the belief: 'I am without value as a person.' If that person forms an intimate relationship her lack of self-acceptance soon shows itself in the kinds of demand she makes upon her partner. These take the form: 'You must love me, and only me! You must show me you love me by giving me your undivided attention at all times, especially when we are out together!' Driven by these demands, the jealous person is seldom free from a strong undercurrent of anxiety.

To alleviate these uncomfortable feelings of anxiety, the jealous individual tries to control the movements or behaviour of his or her partner. The pattern of control used gives a clue to the balance of power in the relationship. If the balance of power rests with the man, direct methods of control are employed, such as forbidding the woman from taking a job outside the home or socializing with her women friends. If it rests with the woman, indirect methods are used, involving some kind of checking up on her partner – snooping on phone calls, opening mail, and so on – usually without the man's knowledge.

All of these ploys are more or less desperate attempts by the jealous person to avoid facing up to the possible loss of love or rejection by his or her partner. The jealous person demands constant proof of devotion and views with horror the prospect of losing it. Not surprisingly, such behaviour sooner or later drives away the very partner whose love or acceptance the jealous individual is afraid of losing.

Over-sensitivity

Jealous people are adept at seeing criticism of themselves by others when none is intended. If something is said which can be misconstrued as critical of their behaviour, they will find it! Even if one chooses one's words with care, the intended meaning is unlikely to be the meaning inferred by the jealous individual. Moreover, jealous people frequently attribute hidden motives and intentions to their partner. For example, a jealous wife, on hearing that her husband bought his secretary a bunch of flowers on her birthday, will accuse him of having an affair with her. 'I notice you didn't bring *me* flowers!' she will say, and no amount of explanation on the husband's part will convince her that there was nothing to it beyond a simple act of appreciation of someone else's hard work.

Jealous people are great blamers. Not only do they berate and blame themselves for what they perceive as their own shortcomings, but they are also quick to damn others for their alleged misdeeds. And just as jealous people cannot accept themselves with their shortcomings, neither can they accept others when these others display their own shortcomings or behave less well than they might.

Emotional blackmail

People with a jealousy problem will often try to get their own way by using emotional blackmail. Because they see themselves as inadequate and worthless they lack the confidence to speak up and say what they want. Fearing their request will be refused, they try to improve their chances of winning acceptance by endeavouring to instil a feeling of guilt in the person to whom the request was directed. Here is an example. 'If you don't bring your car round when I want it, I will have to walk to the shops and if I have a heart attack it will be all your fault.'

Being overly suspicious

It is part of the paranoia exhibited by jealous people not only to be unduly sensitive to criticism and to infer criticism of themselves when none was intended, but also to be inordinately suspicious of other people's behaviour and motives. A jealous husband overhearing his wife talking quietly on the phone will easily convince himself that she is talking about him. If he comes across his wife talking and laughing with some friends in the street, he is likely to convince himself that they are laughing at him. Quite frequently, jealous people will infer from their partners' talking to others that their partners are having an affair, or that their partners must find these people they talk to more attractive than themselves.

These, then, are some of the main characteristics of jealous people. If you suffer from jealousy yourself you run a considerable risk of damaging, even destroying, any intimate relationship you may already have. The same is true if you are unfortunate enough to be in a relationship with a jealous partner. We have never heard of a relationship being improved by jealousy. But we have known several relationships which were made miserable by jealousy and others which were totally destroyed.

But knowing the salient characteristics of jealousy will be of little help to you unless you have an effective way of dealing with it. Let's now look at how we tackle the problem of jealousy.

The A-B-C of jealousy

Look again at the title of this chapter: 'I just get jealous and I don't know why'. That's what some people have told us. They are aware that they feel jealous but they don't know why. Well, our feelings just don't suddenly appear spontaneously as if by some kind of magic. There's always a reason! If you have been following us so far you may suspect that it is not some situation, such as the sight of your boyfriend or husband at a party devoting his attention exclusively to some other woman, that makes you feel jealous. Such a situation may well be a legitimate cause of annoyance or irritation to you. After all, you came to the party with your partner and you expect to enjoy it, with your partner sharing at least some of the time with you. But if you feel jealous in this situation, it is not your partner's absorption with this other woman that causes your jealousy. It is a contributing factor of course, but it cannot by itself make you feel jealous. Your jealousy arises from what you tell yourself about the situation.

As we have done before, we shall denote the situation in which your partner is behaving in a manner which displeases you as point A. At point C you feel more than displeased. You observe you are feeling jealous of this woman who is monopolizing your partner's attentions and you wonder what they are saying to each other. You notice them laughing together. You think they must be making fun of you, and you feel more and more anxious. But, as we've just said, it isn't the external situation at point A which causes you to feel upset but rather your beliefs about what is happening at point A. What beliefs? In typical RET style, we use point B to stand for your beliefs about or evaluation of the situation or event at point A. What thoughts go through your mind in a situation like this?

First, you are thinking a fairly rational set of thoughts. Typically, these rational thoughts about the situation you are in are along the following lines: 'How annoying that he is spending so much of his time entertaining that other woman! I wish he would spend more time here with me. That's what we came for – to enjoy the party together. I find it irritating when he sidelines me and then gets himself involved in socializing for most of the evening with someone else whom he obviously finds attractive.' Thoughts like these represent a rational appraisal of the situation. Your wishes have been frustrated and you feel irritated and annoyed with what your partner is doing. If you stayed with these feelings you would probably confront your partner and seek an explanation from him as to why he had treated you with such a clear lack of consideration of your own wishes in the matter. Depending on his answer, you could then take some appropriate action in the context of how you saw your personal relationship with him developing in the future.

If you really believed that your partner's behaviour at the party was annoying and frustrating but nothing more than that, you would probably not feel jealous. You would feel irritated and disappointed, and this reaction is quite appropriate in the circumstances. Unfortunately, your feelings go far beyond irritation and disappointment at your partner's poor behaviour. You feel all the hallmarks of intense jealousy: fear that your partner is about to leave you; feelings of inferiority and insecurity; suspicion that the encounter between your partner and the other woman may have been planned in advance; and perhaps even hatred of this other woman for daring to be so friendly with your partner. To experience these feelings you would be convinced of several irrational beliefs, such as the following:

(1) 'I must have my partner's undivided love and attention at all times, and if I don't that proves I'm no good.'
(2) 'My partner belongs to me. He's *mine*, and no one else has the right to take him away from me.'

(3) 'My partner must not be friends with or show an interest in any other woman. If he does, that means that there is something going on and I couldn't stand the thought of losing him to someone else.'

If you hold ideas similar to these you are going to spend a lot of your time feeling unhappy, even miserable. You can't be happy being constantly on the watch for signs that your partner might be less than entirely devoted to you, or – heaven forbid – that your partner might become interested in somebody else. OK, you love your partner, it's mutual, you enjoy a good relationship and you want it to continue. We would expect you to be concerned over the possibility of losing your partner. In trying to persuade you to give up your feelings of jealousy we are definitely not suggesting that you should take a 'What does it matter?' attitude.

Giving up jealousy doesn't mean denying the strength of your feelings for your partner or becoming indifferent to the possible break-up of your relationship. There could arise times in any relationship when there may be grounds for legitimate concern that things are not going too well and that something had better be done about it. A little later we shall go into this question in more detail when we come to discuss rational jealousy. Our focus of attention now is that set of irrational beliefs which we claimed was the real cause of jealousy. It is important that you understand why the beliefs we set out above are irrational and why it is important that you learn how to dispute them and replace them with more realistic convictions if you really want to rid yourself of jealousy or to help someone close to you to reduce his level of jealousy to a point where it is no longer too serious a problem.

Beliefs which cause jealousy: how to dispute them

In RET we use three main criteria to determine whether or not a given belief is rational:

(1) Does it help you achieve your main goals and purposes?
(2) Is it logical, that is, does it make sense?
(3) Is it realistic, that is, does it conform with the facts of reality?

If you can answer 'yes' to each of these three questions, you may assume the belief is rational. If you cannot answer 'yes', you may assume that the belief is flawed in some fundamental way. Keeping these criteria of rationality in mind, let's now examine these beliefs which a jealous person typically holds.

(1) 'I must have my partner's undivided love and attention at all times, and if I don't that proves I'm no good.'

This is a pretty tall order for a start! You are demanding (not asking, mind you, but *demanding*) a guarantee that your partner will be interested *only* in you and will continue to love you indefinitely. Ask yourself whether there are really any guarantees in life. Even if someone truly loves you, how can that person possibly *guarantee* to love you, come what may? And just suppose that you actually got such a guarantee. Do you think you would be happy then? We can assure you, you wouldn't! You would be miserable wondering how long it will last, and if you didn't get the guarantee you demanded, you would be miserable until you got it. Either way you lose. There are simply no guarantees in the world, and if you *must* have them, you're on a hiding to nothing.

Then, to make matters worse, you claim that unless you do get your partner's undivided and unstinting love, that will prove that you're no good. Really? All that it proves is that you have a really terrific talent for self-depreciation. For how can anyone make you a worthwhile or worthless person by any action of theirs? Your self-worth, your enjoyment of life, cannot be bestowed on you by some other person; and by the same token it cannot be taken away from you. For the sake of argument, let's suppose the worst actually happened. In your case, let's imagine that your partner walks out on you one day, saying: 'I don't love you any more and I probably never will!' Now, by what magic could your partner's action make you *less of a person*? Unless you were to convince yourself that your partner's leaving you was a horrible, ego-destroying thing, how could you feel you had been depreciated as a person? No way could you feel depreciated *except in your own head*! Instead of bemoaning your situation and feeling sorry for yourself and angry at your partner for doing such a 'horrible' thing to poor you, if you really accepted yourself you could calmly say to your partner: 'Look, if you are unwilling to be faithful to me, let's break up and be done with it. If you've got some kind of a problem about staying true to somebody, tough! But that's your problem, it isn't mine.' All you would have to do then would be to fully accept that your partner had this problem and either persuade him to stay in the relationship and let you help him get over it, or simply suggest that he leave and find himself some other partner who would be happy to live with his polygamous inclinations. Your own feeling is the real issue here, and not the actual or presumed loss of your partner's love. And since your feeling is created by the way you perceive and think about your situation *vis-à-vis* your partner, it is clear that to change your feelings of anxiety and self-depreciation that accompanies it, you had better challenge and dispute the irrational elements in your thinking. Realistically, you can strive to create and maintain a good, exclusive loving relationship with your partner so that he or she would be unlikely to want anything different. But is it realistic to *demand* eternal devotion from someone? And if you did, how likely would you be to get it? Extremely unlikely, we would say!

Once you recognize and successfully dispute these irrational beliefs which created and sustained your irrational jealousy you will tend to acquire more realistic and less demanding or dogmatic views on love and life. Thus, instead of dogmatically adhering to your previous irrational belief that you *had* to have your partner's undivided love and attention at all times, you would more likely tend to convince yourself that 'I would very much like you to love me and to have an exclusive relationship with me, but there is no reason why you *have* to. Even if you don't feel the same way about me as I do about you, I can still be happy, although probably less happy than I would be if you were to reciprocate my feelings for you.'

Once you become convinced that these ideas make sense, you will begin to feel differently about your partner. Your previous pattern of jealous feelings will diminish, and your actions will reflect your new philosophy. Instead of anxiously wondering what your partner is up to when he isn't with you, you will focus more on your own interests and tasks of the moment. You will try, calmly and persistently, to create the best possible relationship you can with your partner so that neither you nor he will want anything very different. But if it doesn't work out as you had hoped, you will feel sad and frustrated, but hardly panicky or distraught.

(2) 'My partner belongs to me. He's mine, and no one else has the right to take him away from me.'

If you believe that you own somebody as soon as a mutual commitment has been made (with maybe a ring to show off to the world outside), you are holding a very irrational, and potentially dangerous belief. Nobody owns anybody else. Slavery was abolished years and years ago. Like a child clutching some precious toy to himself and warning other children to keep their hands off, the jealous person tries to prevent her partner from having any contact whatever with anyone, especially any member of the opposite sex, who might be a possible competitor for the affections of her beloved. Suffering from an extremely low sense of personal worth or esteem, the jealous individual feels quite inadequate and unable to compete with other individuals whom she suspects may try to steal her partner. Most of the time nobody *wants* to steal her partner;

jealous people are notorious for seeing evil where none exists. They do not calmly examine the evidence behind their often demented convictions; they manufacture it.

It is perfectly sane to wish to keep the loyalty of your partner and to strive in various rational ways to please him by being loving and considerate and doing things which will encourage him to want to remain in the relationship with you indefinitely. And the point is that he *wants* to stay. He can't be forced to stay or forced to want to stay. A loving relationship is essentially a mutual agreement freely entered into by two people to fulfil certain specific desires and conditions. If the desired consequences are not, or cannot be realized, either or both partners will sooner or later wish to terminate the relationship. It is totally irrational to demand that such an outcome must not happen because one partner 'belongs' to the other and therefore must not leave. 'You can't do that to me!' one partner will cry, but the fact is that if the other person is going to leave, short of chaining him to a post, there is no way of stopping him from leaving. Trying to keep your partner in the relationship by monitoring the mail or eavesdropping on his phone calls and generally doing everything you can to restrict his freedom of decision and movement is more likely to drive him away than encourage him to stay with you. If you want your mate to love you, try being lovable yourself.

How can you do that? Well, the first step is to accept yourself as a human being with intrinsic worth or value who will retain that intrinsic value regardless of whether you are loved or approved by your present partner, or indeed by any future partner. Nobody, we repeat, can give you intrinsic value or take it away from you no matter what they do. Next, question the belief that you *need* to be loved by someone. Young children need to be loved by someone or their survival would be in question. But you are no longer a child. You won't die if nobody loves you! It's very nice to be loved, at least some of the time, but you don't *need* it.

You've questioned the crazy notion that you are worthless without the love of your partner, and, we hope, are beginning to get rid of that belief. You can also question the equally silly belief that if your partner leaves you, you could never find another. At one time in the past you were without your present partner and obviously survived that. So quite how do you reach the conclusion that you could never find a replacement for your present lover should your relationship with him be terminated? You obviously succeeded once at least in winning the person you wanted for a loving relationship. Where is the evidence that you couldn't succeed yet again?

Now, let's see what rational beliefs you would come to hold once you gave up the irrational idea that you owned your partner: You would accept the rational idea that nobody owns anybody: 'I love you dearly and would very much like to devote myself to loving you, and only you. But that desire of mine does not oblige you to wholly reciprocate my feelings or to feel obliged to restrict yourself only to me. Each of us has a right to his or her own feelings and to choose behaviour appropriate to these feelings. I can accept you with your feelings and still go on loving you.' If you can really convince yourself of that rational belief until it becomes a part of you, it will be difficult for you to become jealous, or to remain jealous. You can still love your partner, appreciate his finer points, accept that others may find him attractive as you do, but not feel anxious about losing him, or feel compelled to restrict his freedom of choice or movement. You love and accept him as he is.

How would you tend to behave given these rational convictions? Well, knowing that there are no guarantees of either eternal life or eternal love, and being aware of the fact that the world is full of competition – competition at every level for resources, for life, and for love – you would make it a priority to make your relationship as satisfying as possible for both of you. If you've created a really good relationship with your partner, and you know the kind of things that turn him on to you, you will probably go ahead and do just that. If you and he already spend most of your time together you're in the driving seat, and since relationships are largely what we make them, you will feel confident and sufficiently strongly motivated to try to make yours so good that the potential competition won't even get a look in! When you are free of jealousy you already have a head start over most of the competition if you want to create and maintain a long-term loving relationship with the partner of your choice.

(3) 'My partner must not be friends with, or show an interest in, any other woman. If he does, that means that there is something going on, and I couldn't stand the thought of losing him to someone else.'

Let's put this irrational idea into our A-B-C framework. It's good practice for you to frame episodes of emotional disturbance in this way because it helps you distinguish the three components of the emotional problem and so go on to tackle the root cause of your problem instead of allowing yourself to be sidetracked by peripheral matters.

At point A, let's assume you see your partner carrying on a lively conversation with some woman. At point C you feel anxious. At point B you are telling yourself something to make yourself feel anxious: your partner *must* not be friends with or show an interest in any other woman. Once again observe that 'must'! Previously, you were insisting that you *must* have your partner's undivided love and attention. Now, here you are again demanding that your partner must not be friends with or show an interest in any other woman. Don't you think that these are pretty steep demands to make of anyone, but especially of someone you love? Can you see that it is totally unrealistic to think that you can dictate the course of someone else's life? We can hardly dictate the shape of our own life, let alone that of somebody else. But the deeper and more important question is, why do you think you *have* to make these demands on your partner? Why are you attempting to wall him off from any kind of friendly contact with the opposite sex? What are you afraid of? Well, you say you 'couldn't stand the thought of losing him to someone else'. But *why* couldn't you stand the thought of losing your partner? Just suppose that it actually happened. What do you think that would prove about you? Would it prove what you have secretly believed all along: 'I am nothing without someone to love me.'? This self-depreciation – isn't this the basic cause of your anxiety? If you have no positive regard for yourself, no acceptance of yourself as a normal, fallible human being who is alive and can choose to live as happily as your circumstances permit, you will tend to feel worthwhile in your own eyes only when you can convince yourself that somebody loves you and that the love you 'need' to be happy will continue indefinitely. We've already pointed out that nobody can bestow worth upon you by giving you love or anything else. But the consequence of believing that you are nobody till somebody loves you is a constant feeling of apprehension. You will feel apprehensive about losing love when you have it, and apprehensive about ever winning it again when you don't have it! Thus you are in a no-win situation. When you do have a partner who loves you, at least to begin with, you will tend to direct your actions towards reducing your anxiety or apprehension about losing your partner's love. Thus you will act possessively towards your partner, demand constant reassurances of his continuing love for you, be constantly suspicious of his contacts with other women in case there is 'something going on', and generally try to isolate both your partner and yourself from people and situations you see as a potential threat to the continuation of your partner's relationship with you. By virtually caging your partner as if he was some kind of prize canary, you might think you have secured your relationship against all possible disruption. Now there are some men who, because of their own neurotic needs, will go along with your view of how your relationship should be conducted. However, a good many men will see things differently. At first, they may go along with your ideas; they might even feel flattered by all the attention you give them, but only for a while! Sooner or later they will rebel against what they see as far too constricting a relationship. And they may eventually leave the relationship when it is clear that things will never be any different.

Perhaps neither of you wanted the relationship to end like that. When it does, we call that situation the 'self-fulfilling prophecy'. Here is what actually happens. As a result of her attitude, the jealous person imposes restrictions upon, or instigates checking behaviour (eaves-dropping, snooping, and so on) against her partner. Initially the partner responds by giving reassurance. When that doesn't work (as it frequently won't), he responds with anger and ends the relationship. If that happens, the jealous person then concludes: 'I was right all along. That proves I'm no good and I'll never find anybody to love me all the way.' The jealous person doesn't realize that her partner leaves her not because of her intrinsic unlovableness, but because of the exasperation caused by her self-defeating behaviour. We hope that this example of a self-fulfilling prophecy will help convince you that trying to control your partner's behaviour, as a means of living more comfortably with your fear of losing love, will often bring about the very outcome you dread. There is really no substitute for tackling the problem of anxiety head on. The key factor, as we have shown, is the lack of self-acceptance and the self-depreciation that stems from it. It follows that if you can learn to really accept yourself unconditionally you will become much less prone to self-downing and the unhappy consequences that follow from it.

We have drawn your attention in the preceding chapters of this book to the problems that spring from a lack of self-acceptance and the related problems that come from trying to rate oneself in terms of one's acts, traits or deeds. If you still find yourself bothered with lack of self-acceptance, if you tend to take rather a poor view of yourself and judge your personal worth in terms of some external yardstick, we suggest you go back and study what we have said about self-downing and self-rating in the preceding chapters. Convince yourself that the insights we offered you can stand up to critical examination. Rephrase them in your own words and keep thinking and thinking about them until you see that they make sense and that the contrary ideas make no sense and are ultimately self-defeating. If you find these philosophical ideas a little difficult to grasp – and we admit that they're not the easiest ideas to get hold of – here is a little bit of encouragement for you. When you've read what immediately follows, go on and study the rational alternative beliefs you can adopt in place of the irrational beliefs leading to jealousy. You will find that they all make logical sense in that these rational alternatives all rest upon unconditional self-acceptance. And that, in turn, will enable you to take more control of the direction of your life, especially if you have a jealousy problem.

Stop putting yourself down!

Over the years you've learned a bad habit. You were taught to rate yourself according to whether your behaviour was deemed good or bad. You learned to judge yourself by the degree to which others approved of you. If you did the right thing and behaved well, you learned to think of yourself as a good, deserving person. Other people with influence over you during your formative years – parents, relatives, teachers – bestowed their approval upon you when you succeeded in living up to their standards. When you failed in some respect (as being a fallible human you almost certainly would), you incurred the disapproval (or worse) of these significant others. Then you became an unworthy person, not only in their eyes but in your own eyes as well. Not that the standards they taught you were necessarily bad; often they were sensible and self-preserving. It was the set of conclusions that were drawn about you when you lived up to – or failed to live up to – these standards that did the damage. So, if you tend to be a self-depreciating individual, don't think it must be all your fault. Even if, like the rest of us, you have an innate tendency to down yourself, to become angry when your wishes are blocked and so on, realize that you were probably given a big helping hand by your upbringing to upset yourself, to devalue yourself, whenever you acted badly or were judged to have some trait that other people scorned you for having.

The good news is that you don't have to believe everything you were taught. The notion that we can be rated as good or bad persons purely on the basis of our deeds or personal traits is fundamentally unsound. We need not repeat the philosophical arguments in support of our views given in the preceding chapters and in our previous book, *Think Your Way to Happiness* (Sheldon Press, 1990). You can help yourself overcome or avoid many kinds of emotional disturbance, including jealousy, if you can accept this simple maxim: Never rate your *self*. Judge your actions and behaviour, if you will. Work to eliminate your poor traits and performances and develop whatever qualities and skills will enable you to attain your personal goals in life. If you can acquire the philosophy of rational self-acceptance, you will find it easier to accept others, to forgive them their shortcomings, and to become less emotionally upsettable yourself.

Go back now to where we disputed the third irrational belief typically held by jealous persons. This was the demand that 'My partner must not be friends with, or show an interest in, any other woman. If he does, that means that there is something going on and I couldn't stand the thought of losing him to someone else.' What rational alternative beliefs can you think of to replace the irrational ones quoted above?

write down those that occur to you and then compare them with our suggested alternatives. Try to see *why* they are rational.

'My partner is an individual who has the right, as I also have the right, to be friendly with anyone we choose. If my partner shows an interest in some other woman, it doesn't necessarily mean there is something going on between them that I shouldn't know about. I certainly wouldn't want to lose my partner to someone else. I am happy with my partner and with our relationship and I will do my best to maintain it. But if my partner chooses, for whatever reason of his own, to leave me and I lose him as a result, I can probably find other men to love, and to succeed in building a good relationship with one of them.'

How would you feel if you sincerely held these rational beliefs? For a start, you would not feel haunted by the ever-present fear that you were about to lose your partner to some other woman, as was the case in your previous anxiety state. You would feel no compulsion to monitor your partner for fear 'there might be something going on'. You and he would freely dicuss your friends of the opposite sex and probably have several friends in common. Since you realize and fully accept that there are no guarantees of ever-lasting life or happiness in the world and that everybody is fallible and prone to error, including you and your partner, you could certainly *stand* the thought of losing your partner some day; you'd feel very sad and sorrowful over your loss, and quite rightly so, but not heart-broken and depressed.

Not only would you feel differently, as we have shown, when you replace your jealousy-creating irrational beliefs with rational convictions, you would be able to allow both your partner and yourself to open up your horizons, making your relationship, and your lives generally, so much more fulfilling. We hope you are now beginning to see what we meant when we defined 'rational' as helping you achieve your goals, in addition to being realistic, factual and making logical sense. Compare these rational beliefs we've presented above and the feelings and behaviours that result from them with the irrational beliefs which create jealousy and the personal and interpersonal consequences that follow from them. You can live with, or without jealousy, and still love your partner devotedly. The choice is yours.

Rational jealousy

As we have already pointed out, we are not too happy with this phrase 'rational jealousy'. If it is agreed that jealousy is in the main a relationship-disrupting and self-defeating emotional disturbance, it seems to be something of a contradiction to talk about 'rational jealousy'. Some of our colleagues prefer the terms 'constructive jealousy' and 'destructive jealousy' instead of 'rational' and 'irrational' jealousy. But this doesn't seem to us to be an improvement, and we shall stay with 'rational jealousy' for the purposes of this book.

Suppose you are enjoying a good love relationship with your chosen partner but you and he are not spending as much time together as you would prefer. Let's say your partner has quite a few involvements in outside activities which, for various reasons, you take little part in. He has business conferences to attend which frequently take him out of town. He has an active social life. He plays tennis, badminton and squash and he is an active member of a hiking club. Most weekends he is out walking with members of the hiking club, which incidentally includes quite a few unattached female members. You occasionally join in for a game of tennis and now and again pop down to the club, of which you both are members, for a social drink or two. But generally, you are dissatisfied with the amount of time you and he spend together, be it socially or at home. You also admit to being a little concerned at the possibility of your relationship being disrupted some day if your partner should spend too much time in the company of other women during the course of his business or social activities. You feel deprived of his presence and speculate about being threatened by the complete loss of your partner. You feel frustrated and disappointed, but not severely emotionally disturbed. In short, you feel rationally jealous, because you are not getting what you want. But you don't go so far as *demand* that you get it. You could, and probably would, confront your partner with your dissatisfaction over the amount of time he spends away from you and try to negotiate a compromise with him so that he spends less time away from home and shares more of his time with you. If talking failed to bring about an improvement to the point where you felt you had achieved an acceptable level of satisfaction, you might then consider taking some action, such as going to live elsewhere without him for a while, or even terminating the relationship.

You will find it instructive to compare the two kinds of jealousy, particularly the kinds of reactions by the parties involved, assuming the above scenario applied in each case. Whereas the individual who is irrationally jealous demands the exclusive love and undivided attention of his or her partner, is terribly upset at the possible loss of love and attempts to control the other partner's freedom of choice by overt or covert means, the rationally jealous individual would react to the possible loss of love as follows:

'I would very much prefer you to spend more time with me and to care only for me, but there is no reason why you have to do so. If you leave me, I can still be happy without you although probably not quite so happy as I could be if you were to remain with me.'

'I love you dearly and want no one else, but you are not obliged to feel you must return my love, nor are you under any obligation to restrict your love to me alone. I definitely want you to, but you don't have to.'

'If at times you treat me unfairly or inconsiderately or deceive me and thereby betray our relationship, I will feel sad over your unloving and untrustworthy behaviour but I will not condemn or denigrate you for behaving in such an undesirable manner towards me. However, I will review the relationship and may conclude that it is not meeting my deepest desires. If so, I will sadly, but calmly, decide to end the relationship.'

If you think along these lines you will save yourself much needless emotional turmoil. If neither you nor your partner see any great advantages in separating, you could discuss the pros and cons of coming to some form of more open or non-monogamous relationship. Rational jealousy can help you avoid the destruction of a relationship you might both wish to retain because certain aspects of it are of considerable value to you and your partner. By contrast, irrational jealousy on your part will contribute strongly to a degree of emotional misery for yourself and create an unpleasant atmosphere for your partner. The end result could be the destruction of a potentially viable relationship with nothing much left to show for it.

How to live with a jealous person

If you live in a close relationship with a person afflicted with a jealousy problem, there are various things you can do to help that person reduce the severity of the problem or get over it. First, realize that a jealous person is a fallible human being like everybody else. Jealous people can be kind, considerate and charming. They can be fun to live with – when they're not in one of their jealous moods. So, what can you do to help your companion overcome his or her jealousy problem? Trying to help someone with an emotional problem is not easy because it requires the would-be helper to have certain traits and knowledge not commonly found in the average person or household. For a start, you'd better not have a jealousy problem yourself! And if you anger yourself easily, that could be another significant drawback. However, assuming that you are not too emotionally disturbed yourself and that you have a real desire and interest in helping someone close to you to overcome his or her jealousy, you might find the following advice helpful:

Realize clearly and fully accept that your companion has a problem. Don't expect him or her to act like a rational, well-adjusted adult. If you do, you will be disappointed, and this will feed back to your jealous partner who, because of his or her low self-acceptance will tend to feel even more upset because of the failure to live up to your expectations.

When your companion acts nastily towards you by, for example, hurling accusations at you or trying to blackmail you into letting him get his own way at some expense to you, don't bother to ask yourself why. You *know* why. That's the way jealous people act sometimes. They don't hate you, they're not trying to do you in. Because of their disturbance, jealous people act in ways which frustrate or annoy you. Just don't take their behaviour as a personal affront!

Once you can fully accept the jealous person as a person who doesn't wish to be emotionally upset but who unfortunately has acquired a strong disposition to think and behave irrationally, you can then help your companion to overcome his or her jealousy problem.

Set a good example by conveying to your jealous companion or partner that you understand what creates jealousy. You will find valuable material in this book and in our book entitled *Think Your Way To Happiness*. Study it carefully and try to keep yourself informed on psychological findings on human behaviour, particularly Rational-Emotive Therapy findings and developments.

Realize the importance of self-understanding, identify some of your own emotional quirks and, most importantly, acquire true self-acceptance as a prerequisite for helping others overcome their own lack of it.

As we noted above, jealous persons possess many good points. Emphasize these and play down their failings. Be ready with praise, especially when they do better than they themselves expected. Show them they can trust themselves and accept themselves regardless of whether they do well or not. Make the distinction, if you can, between rating one's traits or deeds and rating oneself. Convey this distinction and the importance of accepting people as people who perform good and bad acts as clearly and forcefully as you can.

Encourage your jealous partner to do things he may be afraid he will fail at. Even if he fails this time, there is always the next time, or the next, when he may succeed. When he does succeed against his expectations show him he could attempt to do other things he had previously thought were beyond him.

Convey a firm but kind attitude to your jealous companion. Show him that while you will treat him nicely and considerately you will not allow yourself to be imposed upon, or allow him or anybody else to ride roughshod over your own vital interests. If you weakly allow your jealous companion to run you completely, this will merely give him an incentive to continue and intensify his disturbed thinking and behaviour.

The more you act as a good model for your jealous partner the better you will tend to help him. If you are indecisive, slack and lacking in self-discipline you are hardly setting a good example. So, act firmly but kindly. Set limits to the amount of attention you will give your jealous companion, don't criticize him when he behaves badly. His trouble is already the fact that he is oversensitive to criticism! Being over-sensitive to criticism, he will tend to take further criticism badly, especially from you whom he may now be beginning to feel he can trust. If you do criticize your partner, even for some minor trait, you will be contributing to increasing his already strong feelings of worthlessness – the very thing you are trying *not* to do!

These, then, are some of the things you can do to help a close friend overcome or at least reduce a problem with jealousy. Don't be discouraged if you make little headway at first. Being in a close relationship and lacking professional training makes your task more difficult than it would otherwise be. But if you conscientiously strive to understand the rational-emotive principles of behaviour set out in this book and apply them to yourself first before attempting to help others later, you will help yourself considerably; and if you calmly persist in using these RET principles to help others, you may be pleasantly surprised at the results you achieve.

Summary

(1)   We distinguish two kinds of jealousy: rational and irrational. When confronted with a situation in which one partner spends a great deal of time on activities outside the home, the rationally jealous partner may feel deprived of the other's company to an unacceptable degree. Feeling frustrated and disappointed by the other's behaviour, the rationally jealous person will usually try to negotiate an acceptable compromise to secure more of what he or she wants to attain a reasonable level of satisfaction from the relationship. If that doesn't materialize, he or she may decide to calmly terminate the relationship and find some other more compatible partner.

(2)   By contrast, the irrationally jealous person creates and main-tains his or her jealousy by making a series of irrational demands upon himself or herself, but mainly upon the other partner.

(3)   These irrational demands stem from a low level of self-acceptance, or low sense of personal worth, together with an ever-present feeling of anxiety and insecurity over the possibility of losing the partner's love. This being so, the jealous person attempts to minimize the discomfort associated with these irrational beliefs and

feelings by imposing either direct or indirect restrictions upon his or her partner's freedom of movement.

(4)   We identified the irrational beliefs of jealous persons, and showed the self-defeating feelings and behaviours which stem from these beliefs. We then showed you how to dispute them and replace them with rational alternatives and how these led to better feelings and more constructive behaviours.

(5)   We illustrated in some detail how a rationally jealous individual might well behave when faced with a 'jealousy' problem in a relationship, and then went on to offer you advice on how to live with a person with a jealousy problem and how to help that person reduce the severity of the problem or to get over it.

5

'He Treats Me Like a Doormat'

It is sad to think of the number of women who have used that expression and really meant it. Well, the good news is that we are going to give you an insight into why you may have been treated like a doormat in the past; how it all probably started, and why, if it still is a problem, you are still being treated like a doormat. We will outline the probable consequences for you and your relationship if you continue to allow yourself to be treated in this appalling manner; but, more important still, we are going to show you how to radically redefine your relationship. You will see how to stand up and take control of your life, and put an end, once and for all, to this very unhealthy way of relating to your partner.

How it all started

When you first enter what you intend to be an exclusive relationship with a man, be it a conventional monogamous marriage, or a by now equally conventional living-together arrangement, both you and your mate doubtless set out with the best of intentions. At the very least, you intend to be nice to each other. Be nice, be obliging, don't be bossy, put your partner first, love begets love – you've heard it all before, even from professional counsellors who could be expected to know better. Don't get us wrong! We are not saying that you should never be kind or obliging to other people. If you wish to be treated by others in a fair and considerate manner, you should try to be fair and considerate towards them. The world would be a poorer place if we never treated other people with a minimum of courtesy and consideration. And that goes especially for someone with whom you have a close relationship.

However, it is one thing to be kind, considerate and obliging to your partner, even to put his interests and desires before yours now and again. But – and it's a big but – it is a great mistake to become *too* nice, *too* considerate and obliging, and to constantly give in to what your partner wants, while in the process allowing your own main interests or desires to be pushed aside and neglected. You can be nice to a fault, and the consequences for both you and your relationship will be anything but 'nice'. But why does this happen?

Reasons women give for being too supportive

Women give a number of reasons why they are prepared to neglect themselves in their partner's interests. Here are some of the reasons we hear most frequently:

'That's how women are; that's how we're expected to be'

You will recognize this right away as the old sex-role stereotype problem, mentioned already in Chapter 2. Perhaps you were brought up to be deferential, to accept the line that nice girls shouldn't be 'pushy', that men didn't like women who had a mind of their own or held or expressed opinions on matters considered to be the prerogative of males. Fortunately, times are changing. The women's liberation movement has helped women to reject old sex-role stereotypes and carve out new definitions of themselves and how to achieve more equality-based, more self-fulfilling relationships with the male partners in their lives. And we are especially pleased to point out that some of the leading writers in RET, particularly Dr Albert Ellis, the founder of RET, actually pioneered several of the revolutionary ideas which today are central to the ideas and aims of the women's movement, notably in the area of male–female love relationships.

In RET, as you may have seen in Chapter 2, we encourage women to give up taking a back seat as far as initiating dates is concerned. But we go far beyond that by actively encouraging women to strive for a fair deal in their relationships in general, and in their love relationships in particular. We advocate the questioning and rejection of ideas or customs which restrict women to acting out the stereotyped sex-roles prevalent in their culture.

Changing a pattern of behaviour which has become a habit is not easy. As you will see later, changing your old ways of relating to a partner may temporarily create a few new problems and perhaps arouse some misgivings in you as you strive to take greater control of your life through changing the kind of relationship you have with your partner. In fact, some of the other reasons women offer for continuing to treat their partners with undue deference rather than face the consequences of standing up for themselves, stem initially from the decision to abandon the traditional sex-role model promulgated by their parents and culture. Since our aim is to sustain you in your efforts to get a fairer deal for yourself in your love relationship, let's turn our attention now to a consideration of these other reasons put forward for being too supportive and go on to identify and dispute the irrational beliefs upon which they are largely based.

Fear of rejection

For a more detailed discussion of this topic, we refer you to Chapters 3 and 7. For the present, however, if you are afraid of being rejected by your partner, or of losing his love because you are no longer willing to tolerate being constantly taken advantage of, and you make this clear to your partner, one of two outcomes is possible. Either he will leave you because he still clings obstinately to his own stereotyped ideas on how women should behave in an intimate relationship with a man, or he will merely threaten to leave you. He may initially threaten to walk out because he has been comfortable with the way things were between you (naturally!), and because he may feel unsure and a little fearful of what may lie in store for him if you do become more assertive in defence of your own interests in the relationship.

If he does decide to leave you, our advice is: let him go! Let him go and stew in his own male chauvinistic juices. You will have much better things to do with your precious time than to wring your hands over his going or blame yourself for not having been more considerate of his feelings. If your partner merely threatens to leave you, he may be bluffing and hoping that the fear of losing him may be enough to 'bring you back to your senses'. Don't fall for his bluff! Instead, test him out by trying to convince him of the advantages to both of you and how your relationship could be enhanced by changing over to the new pattern of sexual equality.

But if you fail, you fail! If your partner rejects you for whatever reason, it isn't the end of the world. If you feel sad and frustrated by your failure to retain your partner's love, that is understandable. That is a healthy reaction. You have lost something you would rather not have lost. But if you feel really miserable about being rejected, go back to Chapter 3 and carefully read through what we have to say about dealing with rejection in a love relationship. If your former partner indicates his willingness to 'overlook' your new assertiveness and suggests getting back with you again provided you give up those 'silly women's lib notions', stick to your guns! It won't be easy, particularly if you would really like him back for other reasons. Ask yourself, is it worth surrendering your personhood if having him back means reverting to that old pattern of relating to him which brought you so much frustration and unhappiness in the past? If you lose him, you lose him. Does that mean that you can never find another man with whom you can have a good love relationship, but who is no male chauvinist and who wants to treat you in the way you want to be treated? A final word: once you've got over the pain of rejection, go out and give yourself a chance to meet the kind of man with whom you think you could be happy. Consult Chapter 2 for some unusual but useful tips on how to go about finding a man in the quickest and most efficient way possible.

Fear of disruption to or loss of the relationship

If you consider this to be a major problem for you, we refer you to Chapter 7, where our more extensive treatment of this topic may provide you with some extra help in resolving the problem satisfactorily. Meanwhile, your fear of disruption to or loss of the relationship entirely unless you continue to put your partner's wishes first all the time is not too different from the fear of rejection which we discussed above. In rejection you suffer the pain of the loss of your partner's love, and, if you take it badly, you may feel guilty and depressed. On the other hand, the fear of losing the relationship stems from discomfort anxiety over the consequences of interrupting and reinterpreting what had previously been a stable, albeit unsatisfactory relationship. You've become accustomed to routine behaviour in which you have done all the giving while your partner has done all the taking. You haven't been happy with it, but at least you knew where you stood. To your routine behaviour, your partner made equally routine responses. Now you suddenly realize that once you start 'making waves', there's no saying what might happen. Your partner might get cross with you. He might bully and try to belittle you. At this point you feel anxiety.

Your inference that you might incur wrath and verbal abuse from your partner, who has presumably become quite gratified over the prospect of carrying on as your lord and master, is probably accurate. But, it is not your inference that various unpleasant responses from your partner will be forthcoming that creates your anxiety, nor is it the lack of certainty about what might follow from the disruption of the previous pattern your relationship had settled into. It is your evaluation of the situation that triggers your feelings of anxiety.

You may wish to recall what we had to say in Chapter 2 about how people create their own anxiety through holding irrational ideas along the following lines: 'What if such-and-such were to happen! How awful that would be! I couldn't stand it! It mustn't happen!' Let us assume that your partner protests vehemently when you tell him you want to redefine your relationship to allow you a fairer crack of the whip, more time to yourself and the freedom to do your own thing.

Rationally, you could tell yourself: 'He's not going to like this. Tough! I have a right to make clear to him why I'm dissatisfied with our present arrangements and that I would like to change them. If we can agree some mutually acceptable arrangement, so much the better. If we can't agree, we may find ourselves going our separate ways. I accept that the future may, in that case, be full of uncertainty and less comfortable in the material sense than I've got used to. But I don't *need* comfort and, like it or not, I can obviously live with the uncertainty while my partner and I straighten things out between us.' With rational beliefs like these you would feel concern about the outcome of your decision to confront your partner with your dissatisfaction and the possible consequences for your relationship with him, but you would not feel anxious or overly fearful.

However, if you feel anxious – even horrified – at the prospect of facing up to a verbal assault from your irate partner, followed by the disappearance of all the familiar landmarks in your relationship and all the accompanying uncertainty that that would entail, you can be sure you are convinced of some highly irrational ideas:

'If I tell my partner I want to stop putting him first all the time and disregarding my own wishes and feelings, he will probably laugh at me and tell me not to be stupid; then I'd feel like a worm.'

'What if he tells me to get out? I couldn't stand the uncertainty of not knowing what was going to happen to me and all the discomfort of having to start over again in some unknown place. Even if I stay with him, I can't be certain of how he'll treat me. He might refuse to speak to me and I couldn't stand the discomfort of not knowing from one moment to the next what I'm supposed to do.'

As we've shown you in previous chapters, if you want to rid yourself of self-defeating negative feelings, you begin by identifying the irrational ideas which lie behind your disturbed feelings and then go on to dispute them by looking for the evidence in support of them. Thus, you ask yourself:

(1) Does this idea help me achieve what I want?
(2) Does it make sense?
(3) Can I produce reasoned evidence in support of it?

If the only answer to these questions is 'no', you then look to see what evidence there is against these ideas.

Let us take the first of the two irrational ideas introduced just now – that if you tell your partner that you feel your relationship with him needs to be redefined so as to take your feelings into account as much as his, he will laugh at you and tell you you're stupid, and make you feel like a worm. Does this idea make sense? Suppose he does laugh at you, makes sarcastic remarks about your 'crazy women's lib' ideas and tells you you've taken leave of your senses. How can his words and dismissive attitude *make* you feel like a worm? If you feel like a worm, it's because *you* think you are a worm! Nobody can *make* you feel anything. They can try, but only you can let them. You know deep down that you don't believe his belittling remarks. If you did believe them, you would not be making a stand against them in the first place. You can't be put down by somebody's critical remarks. You put yourself down. Even if you admit to being wrong about something you said or did, that doesn't make you a nincompoop, but only a fallible person who sometimes makes mistakes. Once you realize you are not a worm because someone else thinks you are acting stupidly, you can stand your ground, refuse to take seriously the sarcasm and name-calling heaped upon you and assertively act to bring about the changes you want.

What rational beliefs would help you feel and behave in such a manner? Well, you could convince yourself of the following: 'My partner and I are individuals with our own desires and interests. So long as we choose to live together we can share common interests and tastes and help one another to achieve our goals. But there is no reason why one of us must be subservient to the other. Up till now I have put my partner's wishes first and disregarded my own. I do not have to constantly accede to my partner's wishes at the expense of frustrating my own desires and I am no longer willing to continue doing so. I very much want my partner to treat me fairly but he doesn't have to do so. If my partner derides me when I inform him of my decision and the reasons behind it, I will feel disappointed and saddened by his reaction. I would hope that he would be understanding and agreeable to working out some mutually acceptable arrangement with me, but if he doesn't, he doesn't. Tough! He can only respond to what goes on in his mind and not to what goes on in mine. If he tells me I am stupid that doesn't make me stupid, and his acting inconsiderately towards me doesn't make him selfish but rather a fallible human being who has this unfortunate tendency to act selfishly at times.

In a similar manner you can dispute the validity of the other irrational belief set out above – that you couldn't stand the uncertainty of not knowing what was going to happen to you and the discomfort of having to start all over again, or the uncertainty introduced into your relationship by your actions. Do you mean the uncertainty would kill you? Surely not! Why *must* you be certain of what's going to happen to you? Aren't you demanding that you must be comfortable at all times, that you must not be inconvenienced, even when you decide to stand up for your rights? So long as you demand certainty in a world which is renowned for the lack of it and insist that the world must not put too many hassles in your way when you decide you want to change some things in it, you are practically bound to experience anxiety. You will lose it only when you give up your demand for certainty and the irrational conviction that the world must treat you kindly and enable you to get what you want quickly and easily.

Once you realize how unhelpful these irrational beliefs are and you no longer believe them, you will tend to replace them with rational beliefs which will help you to deal more constructively with your situation. Thus, you could convince yourself of the following: 'Of course I can't be certain of how my partner will treat me if I take a stand on getting a fairer deal, but I don't need to be certain of how he, or anyone else, intends to treat me. If he gives me the silent treatment I won't like it but I obviously won't wither away. If I can't get through to him, that will be too bad but hardly catastrophic and I can then calmly decide if leaving him will be in my best interests. I shan't enjoy the uncertainty of not knowing what's going to happen to me if I have to leave and fend for myself, but I can certainly stand it. Life itself is full of uncertainties and since I've coped with life so far, I've no reason to believe I can't continue to cope with it. As for the possible discomfort I may experience for a time until I get settled, where is it written that I must always be comfortable? I obviously can stand some discomfort and inconvenience, especially since it will be in my best long-term interests to prove to myself that I can go it alone if I have to.'

If you think there is a good chance that you will lose your relationship if you take a stand on some matter of principle that is important to you, realize that there is no gain without pain, that life itself is full of risk, and that if you avoid taking reasonable risks in pursuit of your goals, you may wind up with a cosy but boring existence. Do you really want that? Let's look now at a few more reasons women give for being too supportive, too nice towards their partners. If you believe any of these reasons, men may well beat a path to your door. The drawback is that, once inside, the men will behave as if the doormat is right inside the house, not at the entrance. So, let's take a good look at these reasons.

'Being nice will make my partner nice to me'

Or, put another way, 'love begets love'. Well, would that it were true! Of course, we're not claiming that it never happens: love does beget love – some of the time, but not invariably or very often. You were probably taught by your parents and teachers to do unto others as you would be done by. So it's easy to conclude that if you want to be loved by someone, you should first love that person and then wait for your love to be reciprocated. Well, you could wait a long time! Some may return your love and devotion, but others will be perfectly happy to let you give them love without feeling in any way obliged to love you in return. If you are too nice, too good-natured, there are plenty of people of both sexes who will gladly take advantage of you. Well, it's time to cry 'Enough!' It isn't just because of what you learned from your parents and teachers that you find yourself today being too nice to a fault. There's a rather more subtle reason behind your bending over backwards to be seen as always nice and helpful to others, even at the cost of neglecting your own vital interests. We call this reason the 'concept of deservingness'. It is one of the most irrational ideas you can hold.

Deservingness – the idea that we 'deserve' some reward for good behaviour, or punishment for bad behaviour – is widely held. When examined, the notion that we must get whatever we claim we deserve amounts to the belief that God or fate or some power in the universe *owes* us something. Can this view be rationally upheld? We think not. You may be rewarded in some way by the society in which you live for what is generally regarded as good behaviour, or penalized for your 'bad' behaviour, but there is no guarantee that you will receive what you think are your deserts! Apart from the fact that there are no universally agreed standards of 'good' or 'bad' behaviour, the belief in deservingness is irrational when it implies that you *must* get what you think you deserve, or not get what you think you don't deserve. More succinctly stated, this irrational belief says: 'Because I strongly desire to get what I believe I deserve, therefore I *must* get it!' Does it logically follow that because you strongly desire something, you must get it? The answer is obvious. And since we have already pointed out that in the real world people don't always get what they think they deserve, where does that leave your belief that you must get what you think you deserve?

Are we arguing that it is irrational to strongly desire to win what we believe we deserve? Not at all! You can quite legitimately believe that if you work consistently and directedly towards achieving some goal, your chances of succeeding will be greater than if you simply drifted along without any plan. Rationally, you could believe: 'I have done my best to fulfil the necessary conditions for reaching my goal and I'd like to get what I think I deserve but I don't have to get it. There is no law which says I have to succeed. If I do succeed, that will be fine. But if I fail, that will be unfortunate, but hardly the end of the world.' Provided you stayed with that belief and did not escalate your legitimate desire to succeed into a demand that you absolutely *must* succeed because you deserve to, you would feel sad and disappointed if you failed and probably sufficiently motivated by your disappointment to try again, or to work out a new set of priorities. By all means, work hard to achieve your chosen goals in life. You will often succeed and usually gain something from your efforts. But you cannot rationally believe that because you have striven diligently to achieve some valued goal, that you are bound to succeed because you think you deserve it. The universe is under no obligation to grant you anything!

We hope that you can see now that your belief that being nice to your partner must result in his acting nicely towards you because that is what you 'deserve', is untenable. You've tried it and it hasn't worked. You complain that your partner still treats you like a doormat. If you are convinced that being treated like a doormat is a condition you have largely brought upon yourself, you may now be prepared to consider what constructive steps you can take to change that situation. But first, we want to show you why your lack of assertiveness in your relationship will, if it continues, pose serious problems, not only for the relationship but also for you personally. By the time you understand that, you may well be in a frame of mind to do more than merely consider what constructive steps you can take to change your situation. Indeed, we hope you will be fully determined and committed to *act* to change your situation in a way that could benefit you throughout the rest of your life.

Lack of assertiveness

How it affects your relationship

In the preceding pages we identified the irrational ideas which lead to passivity and lack of assertiveness. Even if your partner is far from being a macho man with rigid views on women's proper place, your very lack of assertiveness in making room in the relationship for your own interests will make it difficult for your partner to relate to you on anything like a basis of equality. If you were genuinely content and happy to take a back seat for the rest of your life, always putting your partner first, there would be no problem. That's how it used to be in the western world not so long ago, and that's how relationships are still structured in several other cultures throughout the world today.

But you are *not* happy and contented, are you? You complain that you are treated like a doormat and we've just shown you why. You presumably value your relationship and want it to continue but without the one-sidedness which blights it at present. We will show you presently how to jettison those irrational notions which hold you back and sabotage your ability to take control of your life.

But at first, we are going to paint a picture of the kind of life you'll have if you *don't* give up playing the patsy, constantly brushing aside your own wishes and interests in favour of those of your partner.

One of the first casualties from the chronic denial of your own needs and wants is your partner's respect. You won't lose it overnight, but slowly it will begin to ebb away. Can anyone really respect a doormat?

If your partner's respect for you starts to dwindle, how long will it be before loss of love follows? When you give the satisfaction of your partner's desires such importance that you are prepared to surrender your own self-respect, what is there left for your partner to love? He may go along with your chronic self-sacrificing, but will he be falling over with admiration for you? And if there can be no admiration or respect for the way you unstintingly strive to satisfy his wants while denying your own, what is there left to love? You will certainly not be happy if you lose your partner's love but the bitter part is that you yourself will have contributed to it. The plain fact is that when both of you are happy with each other, the relationship is happy. If only one, or neither of you is happy, the relationship cannot be happy.

A further consequence of always giving way to your partner's wishes is the effect it will have upon him. You know what happens to children's characters when they are given everything they want when they want it – they become spoiled brats. When they become adults they take it badly when they realize that the world doesn't instantly do their bidding and give them everything they demand. You show you value the well-being and personal development of someone you love by *not* indulging their every whim, by encouraging them to put up with frustration from time to time. After all, isn't life full of frustrations and disappointments? Therefore, is it not good training for us to learn to put up with frustrations and the inevitable disappointments we will experience by *not* having our every wish fulfilled? Can you see that by continually doing whatever your partner wants you are contributing to the insidious disintegration of his character in the sense of weakening his ability to cope with the hassles of everyday life and to undertake the necessary degree of self-discipline he needs just to maintain a stable and healthy existence?

How it affects you

We now come to look at the effects upon you of chronic lack of assertiveness, although in practice these will also affect your relationship (and vice versa).

As we stated above, if you were really contented and happy to put your partner's interests before yours, there would be no problem. You wouldn't even have any interests of your own; you would be a sort of appendage to your partner. Some women in other cultures live in that state today. However, you were not brought up in some primitive tribal society, nor do you live in an Islamic theocracy where women's behaviour is much more circumscribed by traditional law than it is in Western secular society where all religions are regarded as equal under the law, even where there exists some form of official state religion. As a consequence of being brought up and living in a predominantly liberal

Western culture you have received an education, and through that education you have acquired certain ideas, tastes, interests, values and desires of your own concerning the manner in which you wish to conduct your life.

Unfortunately, you've also accepted a number of mistaken beliefs about the way you should relate to a partner in any kind of intimate relationship – such as always putting your partner's wishes first, for example. One consequence of continually disregarding your own interests and desires while striving to please your partner is the build-up of resentment. You resent specifically the fact that you continually sacrifice something you value and get nothing whatever in return from your partner. Alright, if you had no desires of your own – if your sole aim was to cater to your partner's every whim, you would feel no resentment. But you do have wishes and values of your own, and the reason you linked up with your present partner is because you saw in the relationship the possibility of being happier that you would have been without it. But you are not happy, and although you may deny it, you resent deep down your partner's lack of consideration for your own wants, and you resent the relationship.

Is resentment a rational reaction? Not really. It's quite understandable, of course. The reason your resentment is irrational is that you are basically saying to yourself: 'My partner *shouldn't* be so totally inconsiderate of my wishes! And since he is so inconsiderate, he is no good for being that way!' We hope you can see that not only is it illogical to demand that he behave differently, but also, given the nature of your relationship, it is unrealistic to demand that he shouldn't be inconsiderate when you have gone out of your way to encourage him to behave like that. And is he totally without any redeeming features because he treats you with less than the consideration you would like, especially since you have assiduously trained him, albeit unwittingly, to behave towards you in exactly that way!?

Once you allow your resentment of your situation to build up, you are liable to feel hatred towards yourself for getting into the mess in the first place. You may come to hate your partner, too, for letting it continue. The outcome of your self-downing may be depression. You pity yourself and at the same time you feel angry with yourself for having allowed yourself to fall into this hole you feel trapped in.

You may try to blot out the self-loathing you feel by indulgence in alcohol or drugs. These palliative 'solutions' may help you feel better in the short term but in the longer term will only make you feel worse. Moreover, your physical health could deteriorate, putting at risk the possibility of being able to improve your relationship were you to decide later to take some action to achieve that end.

Another possibility is that you may just give up and walk out of the relationship, with or without prior consultation with your partner. The trouble with that scenario is that you could enter a new relationship with all your old irrational ideas about being terribly nice still intact, with the possible result that the new relationship would end up just like the old one.

Is there a rational alternative?

No matter how unassertive you may have been up till now, there is no reason why you have to go on behaving like a doormat for the rest of your life. In fact, you had better not go on as you've been doing if you are serious about creating and maintaining a good stable intimate relationship with your chosen partner. If you are ready to change your old relationship-defeating and self-defeating pattern of behaviour, here is where you begin.

Becoming assertive

At the outset we wish to make clear that we are not offering you a course on assertiveness training. It would be impractical to attempt that within the confines of a single chapter in a book. There are several excellent texts on assertiveness training on the market already and we will recommend one or two of them presently. Our aim here is to get you started – to outline the steps you can take to give up your role as eternal handmaiden to your partner and to become a person in your own right as well as a full partner with equal rights and responsibilities in your relationship. We will show you how to overcome some of the emotional roadblocks and the irrational ideas behind them which might prevent you from becoming an assertive person before you are able to confidently stand up and take control of your life.

Distinguish assertion from aggression

It is important to distinguish being assertive from being aggressive. Assertiveness means that you try to get what you want or avoid getting what you don't want without demanding or insisting that others fall in with your wishes. Assertiveness means communicating your wishes to someone in a clear, honest, direct and unhostile manner. You hope that the person will respond favourably to your expressed wishes, but you don't demand, you don't insist that he or she *must* give you what you want.

Demanding that others do what you want them to do regardless of how they themselves feel about it is the essence of aggressiveness. Aggressiveness means that you absolutely have to get what you want and that you will go to practically any lengths to get it. That attitude is typical of violence and of war. It has no place whatever in love relationships.

Remember that others have rights just as you do, including the right to see things differently from you. They are entitled to refuse a request from you just as you have a right to refuse a request from them. However, you will often win others' co-operation if you make your requests in a direct, non-manipulative manner, offering reasons or explanations where appropriate. But when your reasonable requests are refused, with or without reasons, do not pour scorn on or vilify the other person for not seeing your point of view. Your aggressive behaviour may intimidate the other person into giving in to you, but it will hardly foster a co-operative attitude or encourage the other to see your point of view. Aggressive behaviour feeds upon anger. If anger is a problem you would be wise to work on reducing it before attempting to act more assertively in your relationships. Chapter 6 looks in detail at anger and how to reduce or eliminate it, and we suggest you study it before you attempt to carry out our recommendations on how to become more assertive.

Getting started: some possible problems

Let's turn our attention now to some of the problems you may come across once you finally decide to abandon your doormat image and begin to stand up for yourself. As you may have guessed, you are not suddenly going to startle everyone by becoming a decisive, confidently assertive woman overnight! It takes time, and lots of *practice*. And that, we hope, is what you are going to do – practise!

One of the major problems which might weaken your resolve as you set out to become an assertive woman is fear. You take risks when you assert yourself and you may fear that certain outcomes of taking risks might not always be good for you. A few possible outcomes may carry certain penalties, but you will find that the majority of your fears are either exaggerated or unfounded. What sort of fears? Here are two of the more common ones.

Fear of rejection

You may recall that this was one of the reasons women put forward for being too supportive of their partners. We discussed this topic at the beginning of this chapter and referred you to Chapters 3 and 7 for a more detailed treatment of the subject. If you still feel a little bit fearful about being rejected, read again what we said at the beginning of this chapter and reinforce it by carefully going over Chapter 3. You have already seen how to identify and dispute the irrational ideas which underlie the fear of rejection both in this chapter and in Chapter 3. Go over them again and think them through. See how groundless are the assumptions or premises you begin with and the equally absurd conclusions that derive from them. Ask yourself such questions as: 'Why *must* I act always nicely and win the approval of others, including my partner, at the cost of my rights? Where is the evidence that it is horrible if I do stand my ground and other people, including my partner, no longer approve of me or love me? I can accept that I will be inconvenienced if my partner rejects me and sorry, too, in some ways. But it is not a total tragedy and in other ways it may have some advantages for me, especially the experience itself of speaking up for my rights and refusing to be intimidated by loss of other people's approval.'

Fear of hurting others' feelings

This is a favourite ploy of those people who stand to lose something when someone they have previously taken for granted decides to stand up and make changes. If you have been giving in to your partner's wishes over a period of time without ever asking him to grant you a few favours in return, he may accuse you of being inconsiderate when you tell him you are no longer going to go along with what he wants all the time and that you are going to develop some of your own interests whether he likes it or not. A likely reaction is to lay a feeling of guilt on you for being so 'callous', so 'selfish' so 'inconsiderate of my feelings', and so on. Trying to make you feel bad because doing something you want to do will probably change someone's comfortable status quo is one of the oldest tricks in the world. Unfortunately it frequently works. The 'guilty' party caves in for fear of being held responsible for various alleged horrors which would have befallen the other person had the 'guilty' one gone ahead and acted on the earlier decision. A man will threaten to commit suicide if his fiancée breaks off the engagement to go with someone else. A mother will predict a heart attack will befall her if her grown-up daughter insists on leaving home and setting up house on her own. Such emotional blackmail tactics are all the harder to resist when they are employed by someone you love. Yet, resist them you must if you, rather than someone else, is going to run your life.

An important distinction we make in RET is between *being* guilty, and *feeling* guilty. Thus, you may *be* guilty of some misdeed, you may *be* guilty of acting unkindly or stupidly towards someone. These are behaviours which can be verified; they actually happened, and the consensus of opinion in your social group or culture would be that you had indeed acted wrongly in some manner and were therefore guilty of having done X, Y or Z. But if you *feel* guilty, you feel personally worthless, a low-down so-and-so who deserves punishment and is unworthy of any good things.

Now, you already know from your reading so far that nobody can *make* you feel hurt (following rejection in love, for example), or jealous, or indeed anything. You largely feel as you think. Remember? So it follows that if you *feel* guilty, you have created those guilt feelings yourself. Is guilt a rational feeling? Let's look at it. Does it make sense to designate as worthless someone who has made a mistake, who has acted dishonestly, or who has acted unkindly? Is such a person totally wicked? Granted the behaviour is bad, but does that make him or her a totally bad person? And will the feeling of guilt, the feeling that one is a worthless creature with no redeeming features whatever, help that individual to act better in future? We strongly doubt it. The evidence points the other way. Convince a person he is a rotten individual for having acted badly and the chances are that that person will continue to act badly. A feeling of guilt won't help you to behave more morally in future.

Guilt feelings are irrational and self-inflicted then. No one else can *make* you feel guilty. Following the A-B-C model, we designate some event point A. Let's say, your partner accuses you of riding roughshod over his feelings and says you are selfish for insisting on basic changes in your relationship which he sees as detrimental to him. At point C you feel guilty when you realize how 'hurtful' you've been towards this fine gentle fellow who has assured you that he has never had anything but your own good at heart since you met. What are you telling yourself at point B to create these dragging down feelings of guilt? Something like this, perhaps: 'I *must* not have my partner think badly of me. I can't tolerate the thought that I hurt him by wanting more of my own way. What a rotten person I am for upsetting him – him of all people!'

As you study these irrational beliefs you may have observed that they overlap with the irrational ideas we identified earlier where we showed you how the fear of rejection was a potent source of interference with assertive behaviour. The common element is, of course, self-depreciation, and you may recall from Chapter 1 that self-depreciation is also found in problems of anxiety. Having said that, it is clear that feelings of guilt associated with the fear of hurting another's feelings will put a brake upon your attempts to act assertively just as effectively as will the fear of rejection. To remove this, or any other impediment to self-assertion you would go on to point D. Point D is where you dispute those groundless assumptions and the invalid conclusions drawn from them so that you give up the irrational beliefs of which they are the main components and thereby prepare yourself to act assertively in future, with a much better chance of doing so succesfully. You can probably challenge some of those irrational beliefs yourself now without needing to be taken through them step by step. For starters you could ask yourself: 'Where is the evidence that I can't tolerate the thought that I hurt him by wanting more of my own way? And in what way can my words hurt him when I tell my partner that I want more of a say in how we conduct our relationship?' Thinking it through you would come to see that you could certainly tolerate his taking exception to your wanting more of an equal say in the running of the relationship and that if he chose to allow himself to feel hurt by your words, that would be too bad, but that would be his problem, not yours.

What rational beliefs would you hold once you clearly realized that it wasn't the end of the world if your partner thought badly of you and that you weren't a rotten person just because your partner decided to have a fit of the miseries at the thought of you no longer giving him your undivided attention? Your thoughts might run along similar lines to the following: 'For a start, I have not broken my personal code of moral values in any way. In choosing to speak up for a fairer deal in our relationship, I have let my partner know what I honestly think. In doing so, I believe I am doing the right thing, and I refuse to be made to feel guilty just because he feels upset about it. I am sorry if my partner takes it badly – I certainly have no desire to hurt him – quite the contrary. He has a right to his beliefs and values just as I have a right to mine. I will stick to my guns, and when he realizes I really mean what I say, perhaps I can talk him round into agreeing to a mutually acceptable arrangement, especially since I don't want to leave him and I believe I can convince him that a different arrangement could have some unexpected benefits for him too.' If you practise thinking in these more rational, realistic ways, you will acquire a new philosophy and attitude which will help you to overcome manipulative ploys intended to sabotage your attempts to assert yourself by trying to instill in you fears of hurting others' feelings or create feelings of guilt. Remember that other people cannot control how you think and feel unless you let them. And by the same token, neither can you govern the way other people think and feel about your behaviour.

Putting the other person first versus healthy self-interest

We have already drawn your attention to one important distinction we make in RET: the distinction between being guilty and *feeling* guilty. Now we want to help you to make another important distinction – one which is of particular importance to someone who can justifiably claim to have been treated, or continues to be treated, like a doormat. One of the commonest responses you will receive from a partner whom you confront with an assertive request for a fifty-fifty deal after having endured being treated like a doormat for some time, is an accusation of selfishness. *You*, not he, are acting selfishly by suddenly standing up and making waves for a fairer deal and upsetting what had been a real cosy set-up for *him*! If you should find yourself on the receiving end of such an accusation, take a minute to recover from your amazement and then make an adequate rebuttal using the material we are now about to set before you.

By selfishness we mean the exclusive pursuit of one's own goals while totally disregarding the goals of others. The selfish person is really only interested in himself or herself and cares nothing for anybody else's wishes. Would any reasonable person think that that description could legitimately apply to a practised 'doormat'? Even we can't imagine it! Now, by enlightened or healthy self-interest we mean that from a long-term perspective we give priority to devoting ourselves to those pursuits likely to bring us the greatest measure of personal satisfaction during our span of life on earth, while at the same time taking good care to needlessly avoid hurting others in the pursuit of their goals. In other words, we self-interestedly go for what we want to do with our lives while allowing others to do what they consider is in their best interests. It is worth noting that in RET the pursuit of one's own interests by no means excludes an absorption in people and things outside oneself. The fact that we choose to live in a social group involves having consideration for other members of our group and we can hardly count on their cooperation with us unless we treat them with at least a minimum of consideration and to some extent become absorbed in helping and caring for them.

In summary, while we advocate that you follow a morality of enlightened self-interest and in the longer term give priority to pursuing your own most important goals since it is likely that others will do the same, you will normally have a considerable degree of social interest. You may quite rationally put others's interests before your own *some* of the time and lovingly sacrifice yourself for certain people whether or not they are likely to return your kindness. But you would be unwise to make such sacrifices a life-long habit unless you were truly sure that you would thereby bring yourself real and lasting happiness. Accept responsibility for running your own life and 'to thine own self be true'.

To conclude this chapter, don't expect miracles to happen when you begin to act more assertively. Like any other skill, you learn from your mistakes and you can improve with practice. We have tried to prepare you for acting more assertively by explaining what assertiveness is, as well as what it isn't, and we have shown you two of the main fears which interfere with attempts to behave assertively and how to overcome them.

Resources on assertion

What we cannot do with just one chapter at our disposal is to teach you the techniques of assertiveness: making requests, refusing requests, dealing with compliments, criticism, rejection, and so on. However, we recommend that you purchase one or two of the following books on training yourself to become assertive:

Paul Hauck, *How to Stand Up for Yourself* (Sheldon Press, 1981).
Written by an esteemed colleague in clear and simple language, this book gives the reader an excellent introduction to standing up for yourself and asserting your rights. If you want to become more assertive with family, friends or lovers, this is a great book to start with.
    Patricia Jakubowski and Arthur J. Lange, *The Assertive Option* (Research Press, 1978).
Packed with exercises and many RET insights, this book, written by two highly qualified and experienced trainers, gives the reader a comprehensive coverage of the rights and responsibilities of assertive behaviour. We confidently recommend this book as one of the best texts you can buy if you are seriously interested in becoming an assertive person.
    Stanlee Phelps and Nancy Austin, *The Assertive Woman* (Arlington Books, 1988).
Written for women by women, this is a very readable account of how you can learn to express yourself assertively in a variety of everyday situations. An interesting feature of this book is that each of the authors provides an account of her own personal journey to a more self-fulfilling, assertive way of living.

And now, we hope that you, too, are ready to embark upon your own personal journey. The sources mentioned above will provide you with excellent guidance. One other thing: you don't *have* to be assertive on each and every occasion that offers you the opportunity! As you progress you will learn that there are times when it is better to remain silent. And learning to recognize when an assertive response is called for, and when it is not, is part and parcel of becoming an assertively accomplished person. Always remember that while you want what you want, others with whom you relate may often have quite different ideas, and they are just as entitled to their desires and preferences as you are to yours. You have the right to be wrong – nobody makes perfect decisions all the time – and if you extend that same right to others and remind yourself that it is wise to assert yourself in an unangry manner, you are more likely to achieve your goals than if you get other people's backs up by aggressively disregarding their own desires and preferences.

Finally, don't be discouraged by occasional failures or the discomfort you may experience following the break-up of a relationship. There is no law that says that your life must be easy; and any discomfort or inconvenience you experience is likely to be only moderate, never *awful* or *horrible*. So don't give up! Use RET to work on your low frustration tolerance, and *work* at becoming a more self-assertive, more fulfilled person. We leave you with the reply a New York taxi driver gave to a woman who stopped and asked him how she could get to Carnegie Hall: 'By practising, lady!'

Summary

(1)   We examined the plight of those women in close relationships who become too supportive of their partners, too ready to put their partner's interests and wishes first while disregarding their own legitimate desires and preferences.

(2)   Four main reasons which women put forward to justify the over-supportive role they occupy in their relationships were discussed. These reasons are:

(a)   '*This is how we're supposed to be.*' This belief is derived from the sex-role expectations women acquire from their upbringing and the prevailing consensus of their culture.

(b)   *Fear of rejection.* The woman is afraid that her partner will reject her if he perceives her as 'stepping out of line' when she expresses a wish to pursue her own interests.

(c)   *Fear of disruption to or loss of the relationship.* This is a fear of the discomfort, inconvenience and uncertainty which might arise following the disruption of a stable pattern of living and the likelihood of having to fend for oneself in less economically comfortable circumstances.

(d)   *The idea that being nice to my partner will make my partner nice to me.* This is akin to the notion that love must beget love, that some power owes us something, and that if we behave well towards others we *must* be treated well in return.

(3)   We identified and challenged the underlying ideas which create and sustain the reasons given for being overly solicitous of one's partner's wishes and expectations. We showed that these ideas are self-defeating, that they ultimately ruin an otherwise satisfactory relationship and that, from the woman's point of view, they are irrational.

(4) We went on to encourage women tired of being treated as doormats to raise their sights and to strive to redefine their relationships. We suggested that, by abandoning one-sided relationships, women could lead more personally satisfying lives and create more mutually enjoyable relationships with their partners.

(5) To make the desired changes in their lives, we showed that women should learn to become assertive. We made the important distinction between assertiveness and aggressiveness, and then identified two common fears which can inhibit assertive behaviour when you first make up your mind to stand up for yourself:

(a) fear of rejection (previously picked out as one of the reasons for being nice to a fault), and

(b) fear of hurting others' feelings (leading to feelings of guilt).

Each of these fears was shown to be based on faulty thinking which incorporated several irrational ideas. We showed that these fears tended to evaporate when the irrational ideas supporting them were replaced by rational alternative ideas. In this context we made another important distinction: putting the other person first versus healthy self-interest. We advocated that you follow a morality of enlightened self-interest, and we explained the vital point that selfishness is not only the opposite of enlightened self-interest but is also a destructive force, personally and socially.

(6) Finally, we urged you to convince yourself of the value of becoming an assertive person and recommended you to study a number of excellent self-training books to help you achieve your goals.

6

'He Makes Me So Angry'

What, you may wonder, is a chapter on anger doing in a book dealing with love problems? Surely anger and love are opposites? Well, of course they are. We have actual experience, both professionally and personally, of family relationships seriously damaged or destroyed by repeated outbreaks of anger. Without such anger many of these couples would have got along just fine. Anger destroys more intimate relationships than any other single factor. Some relationships may break up over money or sex problems, but anger seems to be the major destroyer. That is why we considered a chapter dealing with anger to have ample justification for inclusion in this book. It is an emotion which can affect us all: *anyone* can become angry. You don't need a short temper or a criminal record.

So let's take a look at what anger really is. Let us show you what it does to you and those you love. Then let's see what really causes anger and how you can handle it. We hope to convince you that you *can* live happily without anger.

Anger: what is it?

At the outset, let's make clear what anger is, and what it isn't. The word 'anger' is used in this book in a rather narrower sense than allowed by popular usage. For example, you will hear someone say that he felt angry over being ten minutes late for an appointment due to traffic congestion when what he really felt was annoyance or displeasure. As you will see presently there is an important difference, which you would do well to remember, between anger, fury or rage, on the one hand, and displeasure or annoyance, on the other. Let's consider how you feel, act and appear to others when you experience these emotions.

When you are *angry*, you are in no doubt about it, nor is anyone else in your presence. Anger produces physiological changes which you can't conceal. Your breathing becomes faster; your skin becomes redder. You experience a surge of strength in response to the adrenalin which is being released into your bloodstream. You tend to kick or lash out at anyone or any object that stands in your way. You scream and shout, and stumble over your words which you can't get out quick enough. In extreme cases you literally 'foam at the mouth'. If you have a weak heart, or a high blood pressure you could, in a moment of intense anger, experience a cardiac arrest which could be fatal. And these are just some of the consequences for *you* when you let anger take control of you. When we show you, as we will in a moment, the consequences for *others*, especially those you love, when you let anger run away with you, it will be obvious to you why we regard anger as just about the most serious love problem you can have.

We have drawn your attention to some of the more dramatic consequences of anger, but anger also has other drawbacks. For example, if your partner frustrates you for no very good reason and appears to you to be doing so out of sheer cussedness, getting angry with him isn't suddenly going to convert him to sweetness and light. Instead, he will probably resent your angry attitude and may even try to get back at you by doing something else calculated to irritate or frustrate you. Then you have two frustrations to cope with instead of one! You will almost always find that responding to frustration with anger, regardless of how the frustration is caused, will make the situation worse, and lessen your chances of satisfactorily solving the problem. That is why we class anger as an *inappropriate* negative emotion: it prevents you from achieving your goals. Another self-defeating consequence of anger is the way it can elicit an angry response in return from someone who was minded initially to respond co-operatively to you. Love may quite often beget love, but anger much more frequently begets anger!

When you are *annoyed*, you experience none of the physiological changes brought on by anger. You don't put your health in danger. You remain in control of yourself. You react to a situation which causes you annoyance by wanting to remove or change it by taking some kind of constructive action. If that isn't possible, you are able to cope with it. If you express your annoyance, you won't use hostile or offensive language and are far more likely to elicit a co-operative response from the person with whom you're annoyed.

Thus, if a traffic jam looks like making you late for an appointment, you might consider the possibility of taking the next exit from the road you are on and continuing your journey by a different route. Or you might be able to telephone ahead and ask for your appointment to be rescheduled. If the nearest exit is ten miles away, the phone you want to use is the only one for miles and it isn't working, or the person you want to see has another appointment soon after yours and can't wait for you, you decide to lump it and listen to the car radio or pass the time in some other way.

If you still have any lingering doubts about the distinction we drew between anger and annoyance, if you think that anger is not all that different from extreme annoyance, look at any recent news report with pictures of mob violence. Ask yourself whether what you see is the sort of behaviour you could reasonably expect of people who were merely displeased over something.

What anger does to those you love

The effects of anger on you are alarming enough. But that's only half the story. The effects of anger on your relationship with others, especially those you love, can be utterly destructive. We are talking here of chronic anger. Nearly all of us have felt angry with someone close to us at some time in our lives. An occasional angry outburst is unlikely to ruin a good relationship. When it becomes a habit, watch out! Frustrations occur in close relationships as often as they do anywhere else. If you respond angrily to someone you live with whenever you are frustrated, you hardly endear yourself to that person. Faced with persistent outbursts of anger, he is likely to withdraw emotionally from you. Eventually, either you will be shown the door, or your partner will exit from your life for good. All sorts of reasons may account for disagreements between partners in an intimate relationship. But unless there is some major incompatibility between them, disagreements can often be resolved if the parties concerned discuss their problems in a mutually considerate manner. However, if one partner angrily blames the other, the chances of avoiding a split are not great.

Since a broken relationship may well be the alternative, wouldn't you consider it a good investment of your time and energy to learn not how 'He makes me so angry' but how you make *yourself* angry, and, more to the point, how to eliminate or reduce your anger-creating tendencies so that they no longer bother you or harm your love relationships? If you're ready, let's show you what really causes your angry feelings. It's not difficult to understand.

How you make yourself angry

Anger can be directed at three different objects: other people; impersonal objects and life in general; and oneself. Since the focus of this book is on interpersonal relations, the emphasis of this section will be anger at other people, but we will also have something to say about anger at the external world and anger at oneself. To illustrate this we will take a typical case.

Every Sunday morning Peter went off to play golf with his pals. Joanne, who lived with Peter, enjoyed cooking, and liked to occupy herself on Sunday mornings by preparing a special Sunday lunch. Sunday was the one day in the week when they could both sit down and enjoy a leisurely meal together. As Peter set off with his clubs, Joanne would unfailingly remind him that lunch was timed for 1.30 and would he please get home in time as it would be spoiled if left in the oven for too long.

Just as unfailingly, Peter would arrive home late – not just by a few minutes but by half an hour or even longer. The meal was invariably spoiled and Peter was always ready with excuses: the round had taken longer than anticipated; the weather had turned stormy; he had met some new members in the club bar each of whom had insisted on buying him a drink; he couldn't tear himself away because the club secretary had taken him aside to ask his opinion about a forthcoming change to the club rules; and so on.

At first, Joanne was disappointed with Peter's persistent failure to get home in time. Each time Peter would apologize and promise to get it right next Sunday. And most Sundays, he failed. Then one Sunday when Peter was later than usual and a beautifully cooked meal had to be thrown away, a furious row erupted. Joanne was livid. After hurtling several dinner plates on to the floor and smashing the glass front of their new TV with one of Peter's new golf clubs, Joanne stormed out of the house.

'He makes me so angry!' exclaimed Joanne. 'He's so damned inconsiderate. I go to the trouble of making him a lovely meal every Sunday, and what does he do? He gets in so late that the meal is ruined. I could kill him!'

Ask people what made Joanne angry, and most of them would reply: 'Why, Peter's inconsiderate behaviour, of course. That's enough to make anybody angry!' Are they right, do you think? According to the views we have been putting forward in this book, it isn't the external situation or activating event which arouses our feelings but rather the view we take of the activating event. Certainly, in this example, Joanne would not have lost her temper with Peter had he arrived home on time. But she did lose her temper. Did his failure cause Joanne to fly off the handle? Let's explain what is happening by means of the A-B-C framework with which you should now be familiar. At point A we have an activating event: Peter arriving late with the result that a perfectly good meal is ruined. At C, Joanne feels very, very angry and aggressive and smashes several household items to make her point. To create these feelings and behaviours at C, what would Joanne have to be telling herself at point B about Peter's behaviour?

When one person gets angry with another, one reason why is that the latter person has broken a rule of behaviour deemed important by the former. A common theme in these rules involves the expectation that one must be treated with consideration and fairness. When that doesn't happen, anger is directed at the person who broke or disregarded the rule.

In the case we are discussing, Joanne expected that Peter would make an effort to be home in time for Sunday lunch, because she went to considerable trouble to prepare it and felt she was entitled to due consideration. When Peter transgressed Joanne's rule, which he very frequently did, Joanne became angry. Her irrational belief on such occasions was this: 'Since I treat him with consideration, he *must* reciprocate by turning up on time. I go to a lot of trouble for him and I do not deserve his inconsiderate treatment and I must not get what I do not deserve.' Joanne feels hurt and she feels angry. Her conclusion based on her demand that Peter *must* reciprocate her consideration for him is: 'It's *terrible* that he treats me in a manner I do not not deserve. I *can't stand* being treated in this inconsiderate way. He is a *selfish person* for treating me in this way.' The plate-smashing which followed was an attempt to show him how hurt she was and to make him feel guilty over his inconsiderate behaviour.

Can you see why Joanne's beliefs are irrational? First, she believes that she must not be frustrated by Peter's chronic tendency to be late for Sunday lunch. We can accept that most women wouldn't like being in Joanne's shoes and that Joanne has legitimate grounds for complaint about the way Peter is behaving. But is it rational to believe that because she doesn't like something that happens in her life it *must* not happen?

Then, because what Joanne demands must not happen actually does happen, she concludes that her situation is terrible, and that she can't stand it. Well, is it really 'terrible' – about as bad as bad can be – to be treated with less consideration than one would like? Annoying, undoubtedly, but terrible? Is it a fact that Joanne couldn't stand being treated inconsiderately? When you truly can't stand something, you collapse! Look at it carefully and you will see that Joanne's anger stemmed from her low frustration tolerance (LFT). You may recall that in Chapter 1 we listed LFT as one of the three main irrational causes of emotional disturbance. Joanne's intolerance of frustration supports her personal rule that because she treats others with consideration, her consideration must be reciprocated and life is unbearable when it is not reciprocated.

What rational beliefs would you encourage Joanne to adopt to help her eliminate her anger and take measures to improve the situation? First, she could try and give up her demands. Instead of demanding that Peter *must* treat her with consideration, she could change her beliefs to the following: 'I would very much like Peter to treat me with consideration, especially at Sunday lunchtime, but he doesn't have to do so. He does what he does because he responds to what he thinks about at the time and not to what I might be thinking. It's bad that he acts in this inconsiderate manner towards me, but it isn't terrible. I'll never like his inconsiderate behaviour but I can certainly stand it. He is not a totally selfish person but a fallible human being who has this tendency to act selfishly at certain times.'

Once Joanne felt she could accept these rational beliefs, she could set about doing something constructive in an effort to change Peter's chronic lateness at Sunday lunchtimes. For example, she negotiated an arrangement with Peter whereby she would pick him up at his club on those evenings when he was attending a committee meeting, which was usually followed by a session in the club bar. To avoid drinking and driving, Peter would normally take a taxi home. By collecting Peter at the club and driving him home herself, Joanne saved Peter the expense of a taxi and in return for giving up her own time, Peter undertook to arrive home on time for Sunday lunch every week, and if some unforeseen event looked likely to delay him, he promised to phone Joanne, giving her plenty of time to adjust the cooking time, or to make whatever other arrangements suited her best. This negotiated arrangement worked out well for both Peter and Joanne and helped them avoid the sort of damage to their relationship which might have resulted had Joanne angrily issued Peter with some kind of ultimatum.

As we indicated above, anger may be directed at oneself, and at life in general. We will deal briefly with those other aspects of anger presently. What we would like to do now is to survey a number of other popular remedies for relieving anger which have enjoyed a vogue in their time, but which don't work too well. You've probably heard of some of them, perhaps even tried them yourself.

Some popular but unhelpful ways of handling anger

Squelch your anger

In this way of dealing with anger, you bottle it up. This is definitely *not* recommended! You may avoid an angry confrontation in this way, but that's about all. You'll feel like a pressure cooker inside. Keeping your angry feelings to yourself isn't going to help you get rid of them. The more often you suppress your anger in this way, the more likely you are to arrive at one of two outcomes, neither of which is very good for you. One possibility is that you will one day lose control and let your anger explode – with unforseen consequences. You may well then be angry with yourself for having lost your temper and thus transgressed your personal rule of never showing anger! This will make you feel miserable, and you will end up with two problems instead of one! The other possibility is that you do manage to keep the lid on your anger but you don't feel better. You can't hide your anger away and forget about it. It stays right there, simmering away and one day you'll wonder what's giving you stomach ulcers, migraines, high blood pressure and other problems. God may forgive you your sins, but your nervous system won't! By all means forgive others their angry outbursts and accept yourself with your own failings as you work on trying to eliminate them; but better still, learn to avoid getting angry in the first place.

Freely express your anger

This one is the opposite of the one we've just discussed. You won't get migraine headaches through letting your anger out but you could wind up with headaches of a different kind. Most people feel good about expressing their self-righteous indignation over some wrong or injustice they have suffered. Indeed, some folk think that if you don't feel self-righteous anger over certain injustices in the world, there is something morally deficient about you! Haven't you noticed how self-righteous some angry people are?

Perhaps you think it's a good idea to angrily confront a person over some wrong or misdeed he or she has committed. Unfortunately, the results will almost always disappoint you. What effect do you think your bitter words will have on the recipient of your anger? The chances are you will be perceived as an aggressive, hostile person. The other person will then either withdraw into a sulking silence or return your angry words with equally bitter accusations, the outcome being a fruitless shouting match. A person may feel inclined initially to listen to your complaint and co-operate with you to reach some mutually acceptable resolution of the matter if you are perceived as a reasonable, unhostile person. But if you jump right in with angry accusations, your perceived hostility will drive away any thought the other person may have had of coming to some kind of accommodation with you. Thus you defeat yourself because you wind up with the same situation as before you angrily vented your feelings. Nothing will have been resolved and your chances of a successful outcome to the confrontation rendered less likely than before you opened your mouth.

A variation to expressing your anger 'live' is to take it out on some inanimate object, or – and this is truly reprehensible – to vent your anger on some defenceless pet or animal. If you 'must' hit something, punch a pillow. The pillow won't fight back and you can punch away to your heart's content at your pillow out of sight in a 'safe' room while you fantasize you are beating the living daylights out of some hated adversary. You might think this is a good idea. After all, nobody is getting hurt, and you feel good into the bargain. A safe and harmless way has been found to allow you to dissipate your anger and hostility. But the consequences for you may not be so harmless. So long as you feel good as you punch away at your pillow, you will tend to reinforce your propensity to anger because you derive such pleasure from expressing it in the safety of the pillow room. You will have no incentive to work at undoing your anger-creating philosophy because you know that when you get angry with somebody, all you need do is to hold your anger in check until you can vent it on the pillow. In other words, providing yourself with a safe outlet for your anger will practically guarantee that you will never get around to looking at ways of living without anger.

Creative aggression

This is another quack remedy for dealing with anger which you may have read about in psychology books which were popular a few years ago. Sometimes called 'constructive anger', the idea behind it is that you agree beforehand with the person with whom you have a bone to pick, that you will give free vent to your angry feelings and allow the other person to be equally frank in expressing his angry feelings towards you. This presumably clears the air between the two of you and has the merit of eliminating the element of surprise: you both know what to expect, you are ready to listen to each other's complaints and neither of you feels put at a disadvantage as might be the case were one of you to spring a confrontation on the other partner out of the blue.

Perhaps you think this is a good idea and would like to try it? If so, beware! In theory it may look like a fine way of clearing the air of the misunderstandings and disputes your partner and you have been storing up for some time. But it will only work if you both can take it. That's quite a big 'if'. You can never be sure how someone – even someone you know well – will react to a verbal onslaught. The recipient of your mercilessly honest criticisms may feel so vulnerable for having his or her failings or weaknesses so incisively exposed that he or she will either get defensive and deny the truth of your accusations, or hit back at you with a few home truths just for the sake of attacking you. Your relationship may survive the experience of creative aggression, but don't be surprised if it subsequently becomes a bit frayed at the edges.

Turning the other cheek

We include this one because it is well known as the Christian recommendation for dealing with anger: 'A soft answer turneth away wrath'. This has the merit of de-escalating a potentially angry flare-up.

The disadvantage of reacting passively is that others may interpret your response as meaning that you don't really care enough for your own interests, or that you are unwilling to stand up for your rights. Others noticing your passive behaviour may feel they can ignore your wants and take advantage of your good nature. People may admire your behaviour, but they will not necessarily respect you or treat you with the consideration you extend to them.

We've now examined several alternative ways of dealing with the problem of anger. You have probably observed that most of them are mutually incompatible or contradictory. Each may work for some people some of the time, but none can be effectively implemented in any or all situations. Each one of these approaches has serious flaws and most have potentially destructive consequences in their application. Not one of them sees the problem of anger as a problem that might be eliminated. They all seem to assume that anger is an emotion that must exist, and can only be dealt with in one or two ways: keep it in or let it out.

Perhaps we are being unfair to the authors of these earlier approaches. Anger has been an age-old problem which has only comparatively recently been understood in a way which permitted the development of effective treatments. The breakthrough came with the arrival of Rational-Emotive Therapy (RET). The insights provided by RET into the problem of anger led the way to a solution to this damaging human emotion, a solution backed up by years of clinical testing and research which has proved effective in helping innumerable people to live productively and happily without anger.

Shortly before we invited you to accompany us on our detour of alternative approaches to dealing with the problem of anger, we left you with the case of Joanne and Peter. There, you may recall, we presented an example of one aspect of anger: anger directed at other people. But anger, we said, can also be directed at oneself and at life in general. Let us now take a look at the latter.

Anger at life in general

Life, as you will have noted, frequently frustrates us in pursuit of our goals. We all have to deal with hassles of one kind or another nearly every day. We try to surmount these various obstacles as best we can. To succeed, generally speaking, we need to have a fairly high degree of self-discipline. Unfortunately, self-discipline is not something we are born with: it is a habit we have to acquire if we want to feel we are in control of our life and to achieve our aims with the minimum expenditure of time and energy.

Acquiring self-discipline doesn't come easy. It seems to be a basic human tendency to avoid pain or discomfort by taking the route which promises instant relief rather than to accept a measure of pain or discomfort now in the hope of reaping the real gains which follow one's efforts later. The basic cause of poor self-discipline is low frustration tolerance (LFT). As you have already seen in the vignette about Peter and Joanne, LFT frequently leads to anger. In that example, the anger was directed at a person, but it can also be directed at impersonal objects and life in general.

Lisa lived alone after her partner walked out on her. The relationship had deteriorated over the last year they had been together and Lisa had no regrets over her partner's departure. But Lisa was angry. Her partner had walked out leaving Lisa with some rather large store-card bills and credit-card balances to pay off which they had accumulated in their joint names during the time they had lived together.

Lisa had a job in a local newspaper office which provided her with her only source of income. For Lisa it was all work and no play. She couldn't afford to go out with her friends and she spent her evenings alone at home working out how to stretch her budget to meet the never-ending demands being made upon it.

In the office where Lisa worked, employees were monitored from time to time for signs of stress. When Lisa's turn came it was apparent to her counsellor that Lisa was angry about something. She had succeeded in keeping her resentment of the kind of life she was leading under the surface. She was seldom openly angry in front of her colleagues, but a few of them sensed a degree of tension in Lisa's general demeanour. Lisa never seemed relaxed or joined much in the social chitchat or light-hearted banter among her colleagues.

Lisa admitted she felt very angry, that she felt she was in a prison, that her life was slipping away from her. 'Why should life be so hard for me?' demanded Lisa. 'What have I done to deserve such a rotten existence? Life must be better than this! It's *awful* that I can't have the kind of life my friends have, the freedom to do my own thing, to go out and enjoy myself with them, and I *can't bear* it for much longer! Life is really rotten for treating me like this!'

Fortunately for Lisa, her counsellor understood the reasons why Lisa made herself angry; while acknowledging that Lisa's life was no picnic, she made no effort to surround Lisa with sympathy. Instead, she persuaded Lisa to examine her beliefs about her life situation and showed her in typical RET fashion exactly how Lisa made herself angry through the irrational beliefs she held about her situation.

She helped Lisa to see that there was no reason why life *had* to be fair or easy, for her or for anyone else. That while it was undoubtedly unfortunate and a real pain that Lisa's life was wearing and devoid of pleasure it was not *awful* or totally bad. Moreover, once Lisa could be persuaded that it was not dreadful but merely difficult and frustrating, she would find that she could stand it, she could bear it. She'd never like it, but she could definitely put up with it.

By persisting in this vein, Lisa was helped to acquire a more rational set of beliefs concerning her life problems. She eventually came to believe: 'My life at home is certainly difficult, but there is no law which says it must be easy. I don't like my life as it presently is, but I can bear it. I'm not being singled out to suffer. Other people have their problems, too, some of them worse than mine. Life is a mixture of good, bad and neutral experiences so I'd better accept that that's the way things are and stop getting needlessly angry because my life isn't a bowl of cherries.'

As a result of holding these rational beliefs, Lisa seldom angered herself over her unfortunate circumstances and soon felt more relaxed and more lively. She began to figure ways and means of earning more money, and got in touch with her ex-partner to persuade him to pay his share of the bills he had left behind when he walked out on Lisa. Thus, by cutting away the roots of her anger, Lisa was able to live with the frustrations in her life and calmly work out ways and means of alleviating them. With her newly acquired rational beliefs, Lisa began to take control of her life. The more convinced Lisa became of the value of her rational philosophy, the more convinced she became of her ability to control and change her disruptive angry feelings whenever they bothered her, which they did less and less frequently. Lisa's new attitude helped her to deal adequately with her practical living problems and opened up better options for her.

Anger at self

People are often very hard on themselves when they violate their own personal standards or code of behaviour. Their self-condemnation can take basically one of two forms. If the violation of a personal rule is perceived as a moral failure, the resulting feeling is one of guilt. If the failure relates to some rule or standard outside the moral domain, the resulting feeling is anger. In both anger and guilt, the person demands that he or she must, or must not, act in a certain way, and then condemns himself or herself for failing to live up to these self-imposed demands.

Here is an example of anger directed primarily against oneself. It also provides an illustration of 'ego-defensive' anger where you become angry against another person whose behaviour you view as a threat to your self-esteem. Here your anger serves to protect or defend you against this threat. Marilyn suffered with a medical problem which entailed her spending a week or more in hospital at regular intervals while detailed blood checks were carried out to get to the root of her problem. She believed that while she was in hospital, her partner, David, should show his love and concern for her by visiting her daily and offering her words of support and comfort. When these daily visits occasionally failed to materialize, Marilyn inferred that this was a sign that he was losing interest in her. At this point, Marilyn would become desperate for some sign of reassurance that she was still loved and could hardly wait for the next visiting period to come round.

While David would usually manage to visit Marilyn on his way home from work by making a considerable detour from his usual route, some evenings he had to work late and as a result found it impossible to call at the hospital on his way home. When this happened, it was invariably the case that on David's next visit, Marilyn would angrily remind him of his failure to visit her on previous occasions, accuse him of not caring enough for her and pointedly ignore any gift he may have brought her.

Marilyn felt hurt and angry by David's failure to visit her daily. She interpreted this as evidence of a possible loss of love (which she thought she *must not* allow to happen) and felt panic at the thought that David might be losing interest in her. For his part, David didn't feel very loving when he found himself being treated with what he perceived as coldness and a degree of barely veiled hostility. The result? David found an excuse to leave for home a little earlier than usual.

No sooner did David leave the hospital to return home than Marilyn felt very angry with *herself*, cursing herself for her stupidity. She did so because she held the irrational belief: 'I *must have* David's abiding love. I *must not* criticize him, or get angry with him when he doesn't come to see me when I think he should, because that might drive him away from me, and I'd find that unbearable.' She then concluded: 'It's *awful* that I can't seem to stop behaving towards him this way. I *can't stand* my stupid behaviour. I'm *no good* and an absolute nincompoop when I keep behaving so stupidly towards someone whose love I dare not lose.'

Notice how Marilyn's anger against David serves as a defence against what she perceives as a threat to her 'ego', the possibility of rejection by someone she loves. Constantly on the lookout for evidence that she is still loved, she becomes anxious when such evidence is missing, and hides her anxiety by a display of 'angry hurt' directed at her partner when he eventually turns up. Her unexpressed thought is: 'You are no good for treating me in this way, because your treatment of me reminds me that I am no good.' Then later, when she is alone, Marilyn blames herself for displaying feelings towards David which she is afraid will turn David off and bring about the very outcome she dreaded. Here again, Marilyn's anger serves to defend her 'ego' against the unacceptable possibility that David might one day leave her.

As is often the case in RET, secondary problems are tackled first in order to clear the way to tackling the main or more basic problem. First, Marilyn was shown by her RET therapist that she could accept herself as a fallible human being and refuse to damn herself even when she made herself angry, first with her partner, and then with herself. Then, by showing Marilyn how to dispute and change her angry thoughts for more rational ideas, she came to see that she could feel annoyed and sorry when she behaved inappropriately, but in no way need condemn her 'self' for her poor behaviour.

Once Marilyn gave up rating her 'self' on a total once-and-for-all basis as a rotten person on account of having an undesirable trait, and learned to accept herself with her failings, she was encouraged to examine her compulsive need for constant signs of love and approval from people who mattered to her. This was, you will recall, her basic problem. Marilyn's feelings of angry hurt towards David were, as we stated above, a cover-up against what she perceived as a threat to her 'self-worth' – namely, the possible loss of her partner's love. Without that love Marilyn felt she amounted to nothing. By challenging and disputing the irrational idea that she *needed* constant, tangible evidence of other people's love and affection, and, in particular, the constant devotion of her partner before she could accept herself as a worthwhile human being in her own right, Marilyn acquired a new outlook which comprised the following rational beliefs: 'I want my partner and my friends to show me love and affection but there is no reason why they absolutely must do so, and if they don't I can still accept myself. They obviously have their own lives and priorities to attend to, and it is unreasonable of me to demand that they give top priority to visiting me while I'm in hospital. I'll certainly enjoy their company but if they fail to turn up when they said they might, that will hardly be a tragedy. Perhaps when my partner sees that I can take the disappointment when occasionally he just can't make it, without blaming him in any way, he may feel like seeing me more often. I'm not a worthless idiot if, on occasion, I angrily condemn and denigrate myself for unjustifiably criticizing my partner, but a fallible human being who is determined to act less fallibly in future. I can stand behaving inappropriately, although I'll never like it.'

Stick to rating only your traits; don't give yourself a global rating as a bad person on the basis of having some unacceptable weakness. And by the same token, don't rate yourself as a great and noble person on the

110

basis of having done well, or because you have some very fine traits. By all means strive to maintain your standards. That is healthy and will help you achieve your goals. Avoid self-condemnation when you fail to live up to your standards. Discover why you failed, try to correct your errors, and try not to make these mistakes in future. If you accept yourself and others as normal human error-prone individuals, you will stand a much better chance of correcting your mistakes and acting better in future than if you rigidly believe you *must* do well and condemn yourself when, as will almost invariably happen, you don't do so well.

If you want to stop feeling angry . . .

By now you may have decided that anger is something you could well do without. You have seen how anger can harm your health; you have seen how anger increases the hassles with which you are confronted in everyday life, and gets in the way of enabling you to resolve conflicts or disagreements in a satisfactory manner. You have seen the disruptive effects of anger on relationships, especially love relationships. And you have seen how alternative suggestions for dealing with anger provide you with palliative solutions at best, and fail to address the real problem of how to eliminate anger.

As to whether anger can be *totally* eliminated using the RET approach, perhaps that is asking too much. Humans seem to have an inbuilt tendency to think and act irrationally. But we also have the ability to think rationally, to think about our behaviour, to check our beliefs against reality and to change our thinking and behaviour when they lead to poor results. We cannot claim that if you follow our teachings you will never feel angry; but what we do claim is that if you accept that you don't *have* to anger yourself over life's frustrations, and conscientiously strive to change your anger-creating philosophies by practising the methods set out in this book, and particularly in this chapter, you will go a long way down the road towards eliminating anger almost entirely from your life.

It is by no means wrong to have intense negative feelings. But you must learn how to distinguish between appropriate feelings of annoyance, displeasure or sorrow and inappropriate feelings of rage, anger and self-denigration. You have a choice. If you want to learn to live without anger, here are a few additional exercises you can do which will help to strengthen your newly developing rational beliefs.

Rational-emotive imagery (REI)

This is an exercise you can do practically anywhere and anytime. It is designed to help you strengthen your rational beliefs by giving you practice at changing your feelings of anger to feelings of annoyance or displeasure while you imagine some negative event – some happening or scene that has triggered your anger in the past or may do so in future. Here's what you do.

Close your eyes and imagine some scene in which you felt very angry. Imagine, perhaps that your partner is actually having an affair with a woman whom you considered one of your best friends. You have found irrefutable evidence that he is in love with her and that they have been conducting a clandestine affair for some time in spite of your partner's constant denials of having any interest in her. Let your angry feelings really come out. Stay with these feelings. You are feeling really angry now. Keep that scene in your mind, but now change your feelings of anger to feelings of annoyance and intense disappointment or sorrow. We realize it may be difficult for you, especially if it's your first time. You *can* do it! Don't give up! Keep trying to change your angry feelings as you imagine that scene until you feel annoyed and sorrowful but not enraged or homicidal. When you have done that, open your eyes.

What did you do to change those angry feelings to feelings of annoyance or intense sorrow? You will find that you changed your beliefs about the activating event at point A. We are confident you changed your angry feelings by changing your belief system at B. Let yourself see what you have done, what important changes you made to the way you thought about the scene. If you found it difficult to change your upsetting feelings of anger to more appropriate feelings, keep fantasizing the same unpleasant experience and keep working at changing your feelings until you *do* change them. You can do it! Remember, you create and control your own feelings.

Once you succeed in feeling annoyed and sorrowful with your partner's behaviour and treatment of you rather than furious with him for being the way he is, go carefully over the changes you made in your beliefs about your unpleasant experience. Repeat the process. Imagine the scene; make yourself feel angry at what happened; then make yourself feel only disappointed and annoyed. Then see exactly what changes you made in your thoughts to bring about the change in your feelings. Practise doing this over and over again until you can easily imagine some very unpleasant experience, feel angry or upset, change your feelings to disappointment or annoyance, and then see clearly how you change the belief system that is the source of your feelings. If you practice REI on a daily basis for the next six weeks or so, you will get to the stage where the memory, or even the actual occurrence, of an unpleasant experience will no longer trigger angry feelings.

You may have realized that REI is a technique which can be used to help you strengthen your rational beliefs not only about anger but also about any other disturbed emotion. Thus, you can use REI to help you deal with anxiety or jealousy, for example, both of which we have covered in earlier chapters of this book. You may also find it useful to use REI if you anticipate being involved in some unpleasant or risky situation in the future. If you vigorously practise REI for several days at least before the anticipated unpleasantness occurs, you will easily meet the situation when it does arise without the disturbed feelings you might otherwise have experienced.

Self-reinforcement

If you want to use 'homework assignments' such as REI, but find difficulty in actually setting aside the time and getting down to doing it, you can use the following self-management method to encourage you.

Select some activity that you greatly enjoy and that you look forward to doing frequently. Use this activity as a reward by only allowing yourself to indulge in it *after* you have practised your REI for the minimum period for that day (usually about 15 minutes). If you fail to do your REI exercise, you don't get your reward!

If you fail to carry out your REI in spite of losing your 'reward' try penalizing yourself. You can do this very easily by doing something you strongly dislike, such as rising an hour earlier than usual and doing some household chore, or contributing a sum of money to some cause you detest. You can also get a friend to monitor you. Deposit a sum of money you can barely afford to lose with your friend. If you fail to carry out your assigned penalty, your friend can be instructed to donate the money straightaway to the particular cause you detest. And there's nothing to stop you combining both rewards and penalties for maximum effect!

Staying in the situation

This is a method of enabling you to increase your tolerance of frustration. You will recall that low frustration tolerance (LFT) is a common cause of anger. Choose a situation which you find frustrating. Stay in that situation and while you feel uncomfortable, practise disputing the 'awfulness' of it by focusing on the irrational beliefs which create the feeling:

(a) 'I *must not* feel uncomfortable.'
(b) 'It's *terrible* to be in this frustrating situation.'
(c) 'I *can't stand* being treated like this.'

Now challenge these irrational ideas while you stay in the situation and relace them with rational ideas:

(a) 'I dislike being uncomfortable but there is no reason why I must not be.'
(b) 'I'll never like this situation, but it isn't terrible, it's just a pain.'
(c) 'I can stand this bad situation, I needn't upset myself over something that exists.'
(d) 'Now that I see that I can tolerate this unpleasant situation, maybe I can figure out a way to improve it. If I can't, tough!'

In conclusion, the aim of these exercises is not just to help you *feel* better, but to *get* better. That is, our aim throughout is to enable you to radically change your irrational philosophies which create and sustain your disturbed emotions and to help you reach the stage where you rarely upset yourself over anything. You can do it if you want to!

Justified anger

One final point on the subject of anger. Some women have asked us if there aren't times when anger, even violence, may be justified. If it's in the cause of self-defence against real physical violence, the answer is *yes*. If your life is threatened, fight for it like a wildcat. The angrier you feel, the stronger you will hit back. Don't allow yourself to be physically beaten or even to live in fear of it. The sacrifice of your life and dignity isn't worth it. Stand up for yourself, or leave as a last resort. Whatever else you lose, you need never lose your self-respect.

Summary

(1) We showed why anger is a problem. Anger disrupts relationships, drives away love, and leads to violence.
(2) We identified the nature and unhealthy effects of anger and showed how it differs fundamentally from annoyance or displeasure. We showed how anger derives from demands we make upon ourselves, other people and life in general.
(3) The roots of anger were made clear. We explained how people make themselves angry and illustrated this by means of an example.
(4) We then went on to consider some popular alternative strategies for dealing with anger. We pointed out their good points as well as their limitations, and showed that none of them effectively addresses the real cause of anger and how to eliminate it.
(5) Finally, we described several feeling and acting techniques

which can be used to strengthen your rational convictions and aid you in dealing effectively with anger when you encounter various unpleasant situations. By conscientiously practising the exercises recommended, you can learn to live a happier life rarely troubled with anger.

7

Working It Out Or Giving It Up

Up to this point in the book our aim has been to help you identify and reduce or eliminate the various *emotional* problems which may beset you while you strive to create and maintain a good love relationship with your chosen partner. Practical problems may, of course, arise in the course of creating or maintaining a relationship: problems of communication, problems arising from differing tastes, interests and values, and maybe even the discovery of basic incompatibilities. In each of the previous chapters we have given you some information and practical advice on how to improve your relationship, and in Chapter 2 we offered you our views on the personal qualities you might well look out for in a man and on the characteristics which would prove to be a considerable drawback to an intelligent woman interested in creating a successful relationship with her chosen partner.

However, the main focus of this book has been the identification and uprooting of those emotional problems which not only seriously interfere with the ability to recognize and resolve the practical problems which can arise in intimate relationships but also can cause much personal distress and unhappiness. Hopefully you have read carefully and understood how emotional problems are created and maintained and have practised the various techniques introduced in this book to help you rid yourself of irrational and inappropriate feelings and self-defeating behaviour. If you've solved your emotional problems, you should now be in a position to think clearly and realistically about tackling any practical problems that may exist in your relationship. The whole point of eliminating any emotional problems first is to clear the way for intelligent constructive action aimed at resolving any practical problems or difficulties you may experience in your relationships. As RET therapists, we are not just interested in personal problem-solving for its own sake; our basic aim is to help people achieve their potential to live longer, happier and more fulfilling lives. Intimate relationships, if rationally chosen and rationally maintained, can be a great help in aiding and abetting human happiness. By contrast, relationships which are entered into for irrational reasons are potentially disruptive of the happiness of both participants. If we can help bring about more of the former kind of loving relationships and less of the latter, we shall consider our efforts to have been well worthwhile.

What do you want in a relationship?

What sort of things are important? What does it take, to make your relationship 'meaningful'? Are you and your partner communicating honestly and clearly? Do you discuss your ideas, values and goals with him? Do you understand how he really feels about you? Are you willing to work things out? Are you *able* to work things out between you? Or would some professional help be indicated?

For the reasons we gave you in the Introduction to this book we are not about to provide answers to these questions. Instead, we are going to introduce you now to several writers we recommend whose books on how to improve relationships on the practical level can benefit almost anybody with problems in that area. These books give helpful information on how to negotiate effectively, how to communicate more effectively, how to make agreements that will improve the relationship, and much, much more:

Gill Cox and Sheila Dainow, *Making The Most Of Loving* (Sheldon Press, 1988)

Paul Hauck, *Making Marriage Work* (Sheldon Press, 1977).

Paul Hauck, *How To Love And Be Loved* (Sheldon Press, 1983).

David Viscott, *I Love You, Let's Work It Out* (Columbus Books, 1987).

These books will help you improve your relationships, but make sure that you have overcome any emotional problems you might have *before* you read them!

Let's suppose that you have used the previous chapters in this book to good effect; you have rid yourself of the irrational beliefs which have held you back in the past and you are now in the right frame of mind to go on to improve your existing relationship. There is, however, something which can prevent you from putting into practice the advice contained in the books just listed. We hope it won't happen to you, but it has happened to other women: the fear that your partner will leave you as a result of your putting into practice the ideas and suggestions in these books for improving relationships.

'I'm afraid he'll leave me'

There are several reasons why your partner might leave you once you start to bring out into the open various points of disagreement or feelings of dissatisfaction you may be experiencing in your relationship. Some men dislike change. Some want a steady relationship which satisfies all their creature comforts in the home, while allowing them the freedom to indulge themselves in a variety of male interests outside the home. It is clear that men of that persuasion might well view with great disfavour any attempts you might make to curtail their activities in the interests of 'improving our relationship'.

Again, other men who are a bit inhibited about revealing or expressing their deeper feelings – and there are many such men! – are likely to be just as reluctant to open up in response to your invitation as the first lot were to give up some of their outside chauvinistic interests. Still other men will give you all sorts of 'reasons' why your new ideas won't work and can only destroy a perfectly good relationship, thus 'forcing' them to leave you.

Actually, we are not all that interested in the reasons *men* might have for wanting to leave a relationship. What we are concerned with here is how justified are *your* fears of being left once you decide to take a stand on improving your relationship with your partner. In Chapter 5, under the sub-heading 'Fear of disruption to or loss of the relationship', we showed that discomfort anxiety over the possible consequences of abandoning a stable but dull living routine with your partner and starting over again on your own, was the real cause of your fear of being left. If you have a fear of being left, we suggest that you go over that chapter again, concentrating on the section dealing with the fear of losing the relationship. Study the irrational ideas which we identified as inhibiting you from acting assertively then. See for yourself once more why these ideas were unfounded and unhelpful. Are you perhaps afraid of being left by your partner because you still harbour one or more of these irrational ideas that may have plagued you in the past? The idea that you cannot manage on your own? The idea that you couldn't stand the discomfort and uncertainty attending the upheaval of your partner's departure? If these ideas, or some variants of them, are still alive and kicking, don't be ashamed about it! Irrational ideas in general don't just wither away overnight. Challenging and disputing them with the techniques we showed you will certainly help weaken them, but to rid yourself of them completely requires practice and hard work. So, if you still find yourself feeling anxious about being left, focus on those irrational beliefs which create your anxiety. Vigorously dispute them. Where's the evidence for them? Do your fears really make sense? Distinguish rational concern from irrational anxiety about your future. Remember, it *is* your future that is at stake here. You are probably reading this book because you *want* a better relationship. Well, why settle for less? The pain of immediate discomfort as a result of having to fend for yourself if he leaves you will be much less in the long run than the discomfort you will experience from an unsatisfactory relationship which is allowed to go on and on. In cases like this it's often a matter of 'no pain, no gain'. But try not to exaggerate the discomfort you might have to put up with for a time if your partner really does leave you. You are eager for a better relationship. You are doing what you believe in, trying to do what you think will improve it. Fine! That will give you the motivation to withstand the inconvenience and possible discomfort you may experience for a while before you finally do win the kind of relationship you are now seeking.

'I've tried but it doesn't work out'

Let's suppose now that your partner doesn't leave you, and that you and he are trying to work things out with the help of one or more of those books we recommended you to consult. You have tried to put their ideas into practice but your relationship is not improving. Yet, you are reluctant to concede that it might be better to break it off completely. If you thought initially that your relationship could be improved and could well be worth the effort if you both tried to make it work out satisfactorily, we would suggest that you try one more possibility before deciding to let go and move on. Persuade your partner to go for counselling. Some men may find it difficult to get from a book the insights they need to help them make a significant change in the way they relate to their partners. In these circumstances a face-to-face encounter with a counsellor may make all the difference. However, you may find that he will only go for counselling if you threaten to leave him. If that should turn out to be the case, you had better show him you mean it! Also, be prepared to accompany him for counselling. Usually, the counsellor will want to see both of you. Actually, you may well welcome the opportunity to see a counsellor because you're thinking that it's time to leave the relationship. But something seems to be stopping you.

'I can't break it off'

Now let's suppose that your partner has refused to go for counselling. Your better judgement tells you that now is the time to leave. You've tried to make a go of improving your relationship, but you've had no success. But something is holding you back. You feel an acute sense of unease at the mere thought of leaving him. You find yourself wondering if you could ever be happy without him, despite the miserable way he often treats you. That 'something' that is holding you back is a behavioural disturbance called *love addiction*..

Love addiction is something of a misnomer, as the originator of the term, Stanton Peele, noted in his seminal book on addiction entitled *Love and Addiction*. If love is taken to mean a cherished commitment to mutual growth and fulfilment, it can only be seen as the exact opposite of addiction, which is an enchaining, autonomy-sapping dependency on some person or thing. Thus, strictly speaking, you can become addicted to a person just as you can become addicted to alcohol or drugs or anything else. You are not addicted to *love* when you suffer from 'love addiction'. You are addicted to a *person*, and in severe cases the consequences can be so psychologically destructive that practically your only hope of recovery is through intensive psychotherapy.

How to recognize addiction to a person

Remaining in a relationship which is dead can be a personal tragedy. The continuing stress will often lead to unpleasant physical effects or illnesses and these may be compounded by the debilitating effects of continuous frustration, followed often by anger, depression and self-hatred. Why do basically sensible men and women remain in relation-ships which they know lack the things which most people want from them – love, caring understanding, intimacy and a sense of content-ment deriving from being in each other's company? Why do these men and women remain in their emotional prisons? They know and admit that it is bad for them, that the sensible thing to do would be to get out. Yet, to their dismay, they hang on. To the onlooker, it is as if these unhappy people were bound to their partners by unbreakable but invisible chains. They want to break free. Sometimes, indeed, they even do, only to give up and find themselves crawling back in despair to the safety of the prison they could have left behind for good. What is the nature of this strange compulsion that virtually chains these people to their partners? It has the hallmarks of an addiction.

If you think you have a problem of addiction to someone, study the following questions. If you can answer 'yes' to most of them, the chances are that you are already addicted to someone, or on the way to becoming addicted.

(1) Do you feel a dire need for reciprocation of your feelings for some particular person and that you are nothing without that reciprocation?
(2) Would you do *anything* to hold on to that particular person, or to win him back, no matter how badly he treated you, or regardless of how consistently he rejected you?
(3) Do you feel a compelling need to see him, to be with him, even just to remain in touch with him, no matter how many of your other

vital interests you neglect, or important activities you have to sacrifice?

(4)   If he goes off on a trip of some kind, do you feel panicky or uneasy? Do you practically sit on top of the phone, willing him to call you? And if he doesn't, do you spend a sleepless night wondering if you'll ever see him again?

(5)   Do you feel a compulsion to spy on him, to secretly follow him, or monitor his comings and goings, regardless of the inconvenience to yourself?

(6)   Do you go through violent swings of mood, ranging from near ecstasy when he appears to want your company, to the depths of misery when he obviously doesn't?

(7)   If and when you do pluck up the courage to leave him, and you do leave him, do you feel so low, so miserable, so self-hating and hopeless about your future, that you go back to him, cravenly begging his forgiveness for your behaviour and promising on your honour never to do such a thing to him again?

These seven characteristics are all typical of addiction. The distinguishing feature of them all is the lack of freedom on the part of the addicted person to take control of his or her own life. Once you are in the grip of addiction, the elements of the addiction control you to such an extent that you lose the capacity to direct your own life. You almost lose the capacity to think straight; what your partner thinks and does is all-important; you are grateful for any crumbs of comfort he may throw your way. You desperately look for signs that maybe he really cares for you after all, and if only you can be patient for another week, another month, another year, everything will then come right for you both after all.

Other problems of addiction to a person

Still other problems beset addicted persons which block them from taking constructive action to solve their dilemma and break free.

Rationalization

A common observation is that addicted persons have a strong tendency to deceive themselves. For example, an addicted lover will maintain: 'My partner really cares for me deep down; it's just that he has difficulty in expressing his real feelings. It's the way he was brought up by his mother. He may say he doesn't care about me, but I know he must! He just needs a bit more time, that's all.' Or again: 'I know it looks as if my partner is cruel and insensitive, but I think he only is afraid of appearing to be soft. I shouldn't expect too much of him after all he's been through.'

Not surprisingly, some addicted persons hold some highly irrational beliefs and unrealistic notions about love in addition to their rationalizations: 'We loved each other at the beginning. He can't possibly have forgotten that, so if I keep reminding him of how good it once was, he's bound to want to get back with me again.' Or: 'I know we're always fighting and squabbling, but that *proves* we love each other! I remember reading that in a magazine somewhere.' If you want more examples of irrational beliefs in the area of romantic love, you have only to pick up a romantic novel or two or listen to the lyrics of a few modern 'pop' songs.

Escapism

Because addicted persons experience more pain than joy, they attempt to take the sting out of the pain of their neurotic dependency by resorting to alcohol or drugs. This attempt to escape the pain of addiction may facilitate the onset of physical symptoms of distress and make their unhappy lives even more unhappy. They can easily wind up with two addictions in place of one.

We could spend a great deal of time delving into the problems of addiction. However, our main purpose is, you may recall, to show how to break off an unworkable relationship. We have shown you how your fear of being left by your partner stemmed from low tolerance of discomfort and over-concern about being able to manage on your own. Now, having spent some time outlining how addiction to a person – usually your partner or someone you would like to be your partner – can cause you needless pain and prevent you from doing what is in your best interests, we turn our attention to methods you can use to overcome your addiction.

Making a start on becoming your own person

First, go back over the seven characteristics of addicted persons and you will discern one feature which is common to them all: an intense need, amounting to an obsession, for fusion with one specific person. That person may be an existing partner, someone you would like to become your partner, or someone else's partner. Whoever he is, that person becomes the centre of your universe. You think of him day and night. To you, nothing else really matters. You know it is futile to go on hoping, yet you endlessly deceive yourself with excuses or rationalizations while allowing yourself to be manipulated and your feelings exploited by the object of your addiction. If you are in this unfortunate situation, or even if you recognize only a few elements of addictive behaviour in your current relationship, you can make a start on overcoming your addiction or addictive tendencies by accepting that you largely create your own addiction. If you sincerely want to rid yourself of your problem, you can help yourself to do so by putting the problem in the A-B-C framework employed in this book and using it in the way that we showed you when we tackled several other common emotional problems in previous chapters.

What really causes addiction to a person?

So as not to over-complicate the matter, we will assume that the situation we discussed earlier in this chapter still applies. You want to improve your relationship with your present partner. You've tried to interest him in the books we recommended as helpful in improving relationship skills such as communicating more effectively and so on, but it hasn't worked. You tried unsuccessfully to persuade him to go for counselling. You know you ought to leave him but you can't bring yourself to do so. He can still be very charming when he wants to, but at other times he totally ignores you and leaves you for days on end without telling you where he is going. Then when he decides to return, you are 'over the moon'. But that doesn't last long and soon you are back to square one. Your feelings are mainly ones of despair, punctuated by brief moments of euphoria when he wants you for some purpose of his own and turns on the old charm which never fails to captivate you. You know you would be better off without him, but still you cling on, hating yourself for being so 'weak'.

In his book, *Love and Addiction*, which we referred to above, Stanton Peele aptly notes that research has convincingly shown that 'it is not drugs that addict people, but people who addict themselves'. Practically anything can become the object of addiction. You can think of 'love' addiction as being an extreme, unhealthy, obsessive manifestation of a normal human tendency carried to absurd lengths. In what follows, we will do our best to show you how we would begin to help someone afflicted with such a problem. But bear in mind that in the space of a single chapter we cannot realistically hope to do more than provide a brief outline of the problem. If addiction is really a problem for you, we would strongly advise you to seek professional help from a competent therapist and use the material in this book as supplementary reading to reinforce your therapeutic help.

At this point we would like to emphasize that if you are addicted to someone, it is not because that person possesses some quality or feature that you find particularly attractive. You may be attracted to that person because of these qualities, you might even fall in love because you find something particularly appealing about that person, but you don't become addicted because you find someone to whom you become strongly attracted. We are not saying that a strong attraction to some person to whom you feel addicted is unimportant. It's hard to imagine you becoming addicted to someone who *didn't* initially, at least, appeal strongly to you in some way! What we are saying is that while a strong attraction to another person may be a contributing factor, it is not the cause of your becoming addicted to that person. So just what does cause it?

In his book, *How To Break Your Addiction To A Person* (Bantam Books, 1983), Howard Halpern observes: 'There is probably an addictive element in every love relationship, and that, in itself, need not be bad. It can, in fact, add strength and delight to the relationship.' Halpern then goes on to add: 'What makes a particular relationship an addiction is when these little addictive "I need you" elements expand to become the controlling force in your attachment.' Our point, exactly. In a moment we will go on to show you where these 'I need you' elements really come from.

Halpern, who treats the problem of addiction from a partly psychoanalytic viewpoint, thinks that the basis of addiction lies in a combination of faulty gratification of our attachment needs in early infancy and the failure of the parents to effectively wean the child away from total dependence to a requisite degree of personal autonomy. In later life the addicted adult has simply transferred his or her early unfulfilled attachment needs to another person who resembles one or other of the parents of the addicted individual in some significant way. In view of what you have learned from this book so far about the interrelatedness of thinking, feeling and action, do you consider the theory outlined above to provide a convincing explanation of why anyone becomes addicted to a person?

While tendency to become addicted may have its origins in one's early childhood, it is not, in our opinion, an emotional reminiscence of childhood feelings of gratification, triggered by some newcomer today who happens to resemble a significant parental figure, which impels one to seek a replay of these early feelings through transference to that unsuspecting individual. Unlike dependent infants, adults can think and make discriminative judgments about the objects of their desires. As a young child you were driven by needs and desires, unable to discriminate fact from fancy. You wanted something and you cried until your wants were gratified. As an adult you can, and do, experience strong desires – for closeness, for attachment, and so on – but you have developed the capacity for rational thought. You can make the fine but vital distinction between desiring something and escalating that desire into an absolute necessity. In other words, whether or not you acquired your propensity to become addicted sometime in your late childhood as a result of your failure to outgrow 'attachment hunger', we maintain that if you are addicted today, it is because you are today taking your legitimate desires for closeness, and so on, and escalating them into mandatory commands or demands upon yourself and the other person.

You choose how you feel! You are not at the mercy of childhood memories no matter how deeply and emotionally charged they were imprinted at the time. Halpern himself admits: 'Feelings from the Attachment Hunger level will make a person an addict only if these feelings are so strong that they can override his ability to act in his own best interest.' Quite so. And what do you think determines whether or not your feelings override your ability to act in your own best interests? Since you feel as you think, you have the power to change, via the way you think, a compulsive drive for a dependent attachment to a strong desire for a more appropriate, more realistically based mature adult relationship. Let's move on now and see how this fine distinction can be accomplished.

As we have frequently pointed out throughout this book, wishing, wanting, desiring and preferring will seldom cause you any emotional problems. The drift of our discussion of addiction up to this point has been directed at discriminating between feelings based on freely expressed desires or preferences, and feelings derived from rigid demands upon oneself or demands for compliance with one's wishes made upon others. Having focused our attention on the compulsive nature of addictive relationships and the accompanying emotional mayhem, and fully aware of the linkage between thinking, feeling and behaviour, we can now identify the major irrational beliefs which create and fuel so-called 'love addiction', or addiction to a person.

The irrational beliefs of love addiction

Can you recall the criteria for assessing whether your beliefs about your life situation are rational or irrational? Just to remind you, here they are again. Rational beliefs possess the following characteristics:

(1) They help you to achieve your basic goals and purposes.
(2) They are logical and non-absolutist.
(3) They are realistic, factual, and consistent with reality.

Conversely, *irrational* beliefs have the following characteristics:

(1) They prevent you from achieving your basic goals and purposes.
(2) They are illogical, and absolutist; that is, they are characterized by unconditional demands such as *must, have to* and *should*.

(3)   They are inconsistent with reality; that is, untrue, not factual, nonsensical or unprovable.

With these criteria in mind, check once more the seven characteristics of addicted persons and identify the irrational beliefs which underlie them. Once you've listed them they should look something like the following:

(1)   'I *must* have my feelings for my partner reciprocated, or else I rate as a no-good, inadequate and undeserving person!'
(2)   'It's *horrible* when he goes away and doesn't tell me where he'll be, or when he'll return, and I *can't stand it*!'
(3)   'If my partner doesn't care for me as I do for him, as he *must* do, life will just become meaningless and I might as well be dead!'
(4)   'The man I love is the *only* man for me I *must* have him. No other man could ever replace him or make my life worthwhile!'
(5)   'Because I can only be happy when I feel surrounded by his love, which I *must* have, I will do *anything*, anything at all, to win and keep his love!'

Beliefs such as these are obviously very strongly held, and therefore are unlikely to be easily surrendered. Moreover, a good deal of anxiety and other disturbed feelings are present when a person vehemently believes, as is clear from these examples above, that winning and keeping the love of a particular person is literally a matter of life or death. Secondary problems are likely to arise; the discomfort anxiety experienced by the addicted person over the possibility of *not* winning the beloved one's reciprocation is balanced by the same anxiety over losing it even if it is reciprocated. Consequently one is in a no-win situation. The quickest way to relieve the pain of discomfort anxiety (albeit temporarily) is through some form of escapism, such as resorting to alcohol or other drugs.

In RET we would begin by showing the addicted person how to vigorously dispute his or her irrational beliefs, both with regard to both the secondary problem(s) and the primary problem. We would also employ a number of feeling and acting techniques together with the disputing methods with which you are now familiar to reinforce the addicted person's efforts to acquire a different, more rational outlook on her love life and her life in general. As we indicated above, we cannot hope to present you in a single chapter with an adequate account of the RET treatment process we would employ with someone with a severe problem of 'love' addiction. We will, however, present you with an outline of some of the methods you can employ yourself if addiction to a person is holding you back from breaking off a relationship which is doing you no good and is only likely to get worse.

Disputing your irrational beliefs

If you actively and persistently dispute those irrational beliefs which create your addictive tendencies along the lines we have showed you in previous chapters, you will tend to weaken their grip and eventually relinquish them as you replace them with more rational convictions. To the extent that you succeed in doing so, your addictive feelings and behaviour will tend to diminish in intensity, duration and frequency. We will show you in a moment a number of emotive and behavioural methods you can use to reinforce your determined efforts to rethink and eliminate your irrational beliefs and replace them with rational, emotionally healthier convictions.

Meanwhile you can dispute your irrational beliefs by asking yourself the following questions: Where is the evidence that your partner *must* reciprocate your feelings? Can you prove that you would rate as a no-good, undeserving person if your feelings were not reciprocated?

You should be able to see that there is no evidence for your demand that your partner *must* love you in return. If there were some law of the universe that your partner *must* love you, there would be no way he could do otherwise. Since there appears to be considerable room for doubt that he really does love you, such a law of the universe clearly does not exist. It may be *your* law that he *must* love you, but it looks as if whoever controls the universe has no intention of obeying your law! And on what do you base your claim that without this particular person's love, you are no good or deserving of any happiness? If you were really a no-good person without this person's love, wouldn't that mean that you were always a no-good individual because there was a time when you didn't even know him, and consequently could not have been loved by him? And if you were a rotten person wouldn't that mean that you had some *essence* of rottenness, that you could never be anything else but a rotten, no-good person? How could this ever be proved? The answer is, it couldn't; so why believe it? What you call your 'self' is not a static entity but an ongoing, ever-changing process. Your acts, your traits, may be rated according to how well they meet some standard related to your goals and values, but you, the person who does these acts and has these traits cannot be given a global rating. In addition, while it is healthy for you to believe that it is preferable for you to have your feelings for your partner reciprocated, it is illogical and inconsistent with reality for you to believe that he *must* do so. And your demand that he *must* do so will only lead to self-defeating emotions such as anxiety and depression.

In a similar way, you can dispute the validity of the remaining irrational beliefs listed above. Ask yourself the following questions: What evidence is there that this idea or statement is true? Does it make sense? Is it logical? If I accepted it as true could it get me into trouble and possibly prevent me from achieving my basic goals and purposes?

Rational alternative beliefs of non-addicted persons

If you persevere with disputing these irrational beliefs you will weaken them to the point where you no longer believe them. At the same time you will be acquiring a new way of looking at your relationship. You will start to see things in a different light as your irrational beliefs give way to more realistic, more logical and practical beliefs, such as the following:

(1) 'I would like my partner to reciprocate my feelings, but he doesn't *have* to. He feels as he thinks and he has the right to think whatever he chooses, like anyone else. How he chooses to feel towards me cannot in any way enhance or devalue my worth to myself as a human being. If he doesn't reciprocate my feelings, that is bad, but not the end of the world and I can still choose to accept myself as a fallible human being whether or not he loves me.'

(2) 'I may be inconvenienced when he goes off somewhere without telling me where he'll be, or when he'll return, but I can stand it, even if I never like it. I can also choose to stay and accept the situation, or I can leave him.'

(3) 'Neither my partner nor anyone else can *make* my life meaningful for me. Meaning and purpose are attributes I give to my own life and they are related to my goals and values which I choose to live by. No one else can validate my existence for me. I may be happier if he cares for me but I can still be happy if he does not.'

(4) 'It is nonsense to believe that the man I love is the *only* man I could ever love, and I don't *need* him although I do *want* him. If it were true that the man I love is the only man I could ever love, the chances of meeting that one man among the hundreds of millions of men who exist in the world would be infinitesimal. Love between any two people would be extremely rare. Since people frequently love, and repeat love with several individuals during their lifetimes, I have as good a chance as anyone else of finding a suitable new partner should I lose, or decide to leave, my present partner.'

(5) 'I can certainly find happiness in a number of ways whether my partner loves me or not. I would like to be loved but it isn't a dire necessity, and therefore I would be very foolish to put my personal

health or safety at risk by acting as if winning my partner's love, or anyone else's love, was a matter of life and death.'

The more vigorously and persistently you practise disputing your irrational beliefs, the sooner they will lose their power to make you react emotionally and behave in inappropriate and self-defeating ways. Once you really convince yourself of your new philosophy, you will come to realize that the worst things that could happen to you are various kinds and degrees of inconvenience and hassle, but no horrors. The following are a few of the methods you can use to strengthen your new more rational convictions and to enjoy a more emotionally satisfying life.

Use of coping statements

Write down on a postcard of a size you can conveniently carry in a wallet or handbag a number of rational self-statements and keep repeating them until you truly believe them and they spring to mind automatically. Typical statements to help you over the addiction problem are:

(a) 'I would like my partner to reciprocate my feelings, but I don't *need* him to do so, and it isn't the end of the world if he doesn't!'
(b) 'There are only inconveniences and hassles in life, but no unbearable horrors. I can stand the disadvantages if I decide to stay in the relationship and I can stand the inconveniences of leaving if I decide it's time to go.'
(c) 'Nobody makes my life meaningful for me. Instead I choose what is meaningful for me in terms of my goals and purposes.'
(d) 'There is not one and only one right partner with whom I can be happy. I can love and be loved by many other potential partners.'
(e) 'Even if I never find a partner to share my love, I can still find ways to live happily on my own if I choose to do so.'

Distraction techniques

You can use relaxation methods and yoga techniques to divert you from thinking constantly about your partner. These techniques will help to calm you down but they do tend to be palliative rather than curative. You will find that these methods will give you best results if you combine them with disputing your irrational beliefs. Without disput-ing, and used on their own, these distraction techniques will tend to sidetrack you and enable you to cover up your underlying anxiety instead of minimizing or ridding yourself of it. Your aim in all these exercises is not just to *feel* better, but to *get* better.

Caring for others

If you still find yourself obsessed with thoughts of your partner from whom you are trying to break away, involving yourself in caring for others can help you to become less obsessive. For example, you can undertake voluntary work in a hospital or old people's home; or, you can offer your services to an organization dedicated to looking after sick and homeless animals.

Referenting

If you still feel overattached to your partner and are finding it difficult to break free, write down a list of all the disadvantages you endure and would continue to endure if you remained in the relationship. Then write down the advantages of becoming involved in some outside activity or interest, such as the opportunity to meet new people, make new friends, acquire new skills, etc. By keeping these comparisons in mind and reviewing them from time to time, you can help to lever yourself away from your preoccupation with your addiction.

Accept yourself!

No matter how ineffective you may have been in trying to break away from your addictive relationship, you are not a stupid or worthless person. You can dispute your self-downing irrational beliefs by asking yourself: 'Where is the evidence that compulsively staying in a bad relationship automatically makes me a stupid or worthless person?' When you can see that there is no evidence for such an irrational belief, you can accept yourself in spite of your foolish behaviour as a fallible human being who sometimes behaves ineffectually, but who in no way can be rated as a stupid or worthless or ineffectual person. Remember, you are not your acts, traits or performances. You are you. Once you fully and unconditionally accept yourself as a fallible human being with a right to happiness, you then give yourself the chance to return to working persistently and conscientiously to undermine and surrender the irrational beliefs which lie at the core of your primary problem of addiction or overattachment to a person.

These then, are a few of the methods you can use to help yourself, either alone or as a back-up to professional counselling, to rid yourself of a compulsive over-attachment to a person from whom you wish to break free. In what follows we shall assume that you have overcome the emotional problems which prevented you from leaving an unsatisfactory relationship and that you are now ready to consider the next steps. What you have learned so far has been designed to help you to risk loving again without falling into the painful trap of an addictive relationship.

Rational and irrational reasons for breaking off a relationship

Rational reasons

Generally, you will want to break off the relationship because your desires are not being met in some particular way, or because you are unable to meet your partner's needs in that way. Any number of factors may lie at the root of this, such as sex, love, companionship and money.

If your partner is emotionally disturbed in some way, and refuses to seek help with his problem you can legitimately consider leaving him. There is no reason why you should have to put up with someone who is frequently hostile, easily enrages himself, or is insecure. Note that we said 'if your *partner* is emotionally disturbed'. If *you* are the one who is disturbed, then that would constitute an irrational reason, not a rational or legitimate reason, for breaking off the relationship.

There are several good books on the subject which look in detail at the reasons for breaking off a relationship. For example, *Marital Myths*, by Dr Arnold A. Lazarus (Impact Publishers, 1985), is well worth reading. Our main interest here is to examine two major irrational or illegitimate reasons why people sometimes break off a relationship. If the relationship is potentially a good one, it obviously does not serve the best interests of the partners involved if the relationship is disrupted for reasons which the couple might well regret later.

So let's be quite clear about it. If you have good reasons for leaving the relationship, you have the right to ask yourself whether it is worth the effort to stay in the situation. If your partner is too emotionally disturbed and either refuses to go for counselling or remains emotionally disturbed in spite of it, you may conclude there is really no point in remaining in the relationship. However, if you yourself are contemplating leaving the relationship because you feel angry or guilty or emotionally disturbed in some other way, you may be doing yourself and your partner a disservice. Not only that, but you run the risk of taking your emotional problems into some other new relationship with the same likely outcome. In other words, if you break off a relationship, do it for real reasons: you and your partner have real differences of a basic kind which are unlikely to be resolved. Don't break off because you are angry or horrified to discover that you do have differences, some of which you might well be able to resolve without too much difficulty. Let's turn our attention now to a consideration of these two irrational reasons for breaking off a relationship.

Irrational reasons

'He keeps hurting me intentionally!'

When your partner treats you inconsiderately in some way, and assuming he is not a psychopath, you sometimes tend to attribute intention to him. 'You hurt me! You did that intentionally!' Well, maybe he did intentionally do something to hurt you, or deprive you, or fail to keep a promise – occasionally! But unless he is pretty emotionally disturbed himself, the chances are he just behaves stupidly or thoughtlessly sometimes. By attributing continuing intention to hurt you, you make yourself angry and then tell him off. You had better acknowledge your anger, but you don't have to express it! Coming out with 'You stupid nincompoop, look what you've done!' may make you feel good momentarily, but will hardly help him keep calm. Before you know it, a shouting match ensues. Allow for the fact that your partner is a fallible human who will often make mistakes, forget to do things he promised to do, and in various ways frustrate you. Don't always read into his actions unkind motives or hurtful intentions. If you do, you will often be wrong, and your partner will then react to your 'unfair' accusations with resentment which may motivate him to really get his own back at you! If you still feel angry, study the anti-anger methods we showed you in Chapter 6 and calm down. Chronic anger constantly expressed probably harms more intimate relationships than any other single factor.

Once you are in a better frame of mind you will be in a better position to talk to your partner about your appropriate feelings about his inconsiderate behaviour. However, if he takes no notice and persists in being inconsiderate and this behaviour dominates the relationship, it's time to leave.

'He is not perfect'

Many relationships don't work out too well. This is partly because people tend to have unrealistic expectations about how their love relationships are going to turn out. At the beginning we attribute perfection to our partners: we expect them to be perfect lovers, perfect companions, perfect providers and heaven knows what else. This is highly irrational. Why? Because when you expect your partner to treat you perfectly, your expectation really amounts to a demand that he *must* do so. Even if at the outset you and your partner were reasonably well matched over a range of attributes, abilities and qualities you deemed important, by demanding that he meets your expectations you are failing to allow for the fact that he is a normal, fallible human being. You probably pay lip-service to the proposition that 'no man is perfect',

132

but when you think of *your* partner or prospective partner, well, that's different! You don't explicitly say so, but you implicitly believe that somehow *this* man will surmount the normal human failings and justify your irrational expectations of him in all respects.

But it doesn't work out that way, does it? Sooner or later you discover that, like every other man, he has his flaws. What's more, you and he soon discover that you are not even all that well matched. In the heady flush of romance when you first met, you didn't even think of checking on whether he was emotionally stable, or ambitious to get ahead, or was possessed of any of several other qualities you could have mentioned as important to you when selecting a partner and potential mate.

When you realize he is a normal human being with some good qualities, some bad and some neutral, you feel cheated. Perhaps you blame yourself for not having made a better choice. Yet, because of your perfectionist attitude you fail to see that once you feel strongly attracted to a man, you automatically begin to endow him with all those lovely qualities you demand your perfect man *must* have, but which this imperfect being doesn't have, and can't have!

The answer? Surrender your perfectionist demands! If you're trying to decide if you should leave him, decide on the basis of the attributes and qualities he actually possesses. Draw up a balance sheet, then ask yourself if your partner meets most of your important desires and requirements. You can then decide on that more realistic basis whether to remain in the relationship or leave. By adopting these criteria you are more likely to let your partner see that your down-to-earth attitude is more sensible and less threatening to him than if you hurl accusations at him of being disappointing, a fraud or some other kind of failure because he failed to live up to your absurd standards of perfection. From this down-to-earth attitude you will also be best placed to negotiate changes with your partner. However, if he just won't work with you to help make the relationship better, then maybe it is time to call it a day.

Now that you're ready to go . . .

We hope that by now you have overcome those irrational emotional impediments to breaking off an unworkable relationship which this chapter has largely been about. We also hope that you are able to leave without anger or guilt. Once you've made up your mind, leave! Don't dither. You can still maintain a friendly contact with your ex-partner, if you wish, for practical reasons. There is no need to part in a spirit of recrimination or remorse, and you won't if you have carried the advice given you in this book into practice.

You are free now. Make the most of it!

Summary

(1)   We dealt with the emotional problems which may interfere with your decision to remain in or leave a relationship.

(2)   We recommended a number of books which contain sound practical guidance on how to make relationships work and what to do if your relationship is not working.

(3)   The fear of being left was treated at some length and the way to overcome this fear was explained.

(4)   We went on to tackle the problem of addiction to a person. We identified the irrational philosophies which underlie addiction in general, and addiction to a person in particular. We set out the major characteristics of addicted persons and tied these into the irrational beliefs which addict one person to another. We discussed views concerning the origin of so-called 'love addiction' and pressed the view that regardless of how one's addiction may have originated, it was essentially self-created and maintained today by the addicted person's unrealistic views about love.

(5)   After presenting you with rational alternatives to the beliefs behind addiction, we suggested you carry out several strategies designed to help you cope with your transition from addicted dependency to taking control of your own life.

(6)   Finally, we discussed both sound and unsound reasons for terminating a relationship. Once your decision to break off your relationship was made, we showed you how to proceed with the break without anger, guilt or shame.